Anngwyn St. Just

Relative Balance in an Unstable World

Revised Edition

Also by Anngwyn St. Just

Fire in the Madhouse 2017, Createspace USA

Lightning on the Horizon 2016, Createspace USA

At Paradigm's Edge: Trauma and the Human Condition III 2014, Createspace USA

Waking to the Sound of Thunder: Trauma and the Human Condition II 2013, Createspace USA

Trauma and the Human Condition: Notes from the International Field 2012, Createspace USA

Trauma: Time Space and Fractals : A Systemic Perspective on Individual, Social and Global Trauma 2012, Createspace USA

A Question of Balance: A Systemic Approach to Understanding and Resolving Trauma 2009, Createspace USA

Relative Balance in an Unstable World: A Search for New Models for Trauma Education and Recovery 2006,Carl-Auer Verlag, Heidelberg, Germany

In Translation:

Trauma: Tiempo, Espacio y Fractales Editorial Alma Lepik, Buenos Aires, Argentina,2012

Trauma : Una cuestion de equilibrio: Un abordaje sistemico para la comprension y resolucion, Editorial Alma Lepik, Buenos Aires, Argentina ,2011

Equilibrio relativo en un mundo inestable: Una investigacion sobre Educacion de Trauma y Recuperacion ,2nd ed. Editorial Alma Lepik, Buenos Aires, Argentina,2011

Sociales Trauma : Balance finden in einer unsicheren Welt Kosel Verlag/Random House, Munchen, Deutchland , 2005

ISBN-10:1723531529 ISBN-13:978-1723531521

TABLE OF CONTENTS

This edition is dedicated
to the memory of
Dr. Valery Mikhailovsky

FORWARD

"I live my life in ever widening circles
That reach across the world
I may never complete the last one
But I give myself to it ."
(Ranier Maria Rilke)

Well into my seventh decade now, I look back with gratitude at this first book which came into being at a time when my understanding of a need for cross cultural, collective trauma work was at its inception. As a new author I received much needed support and guidance, as I set forth in my introduction for the first edition, all of which is still relevant, and later from editors in the German, Spanish and other language editions.

At the time of writing the first edition published in Germany, through the auspices of Gunthard Weber's, Carl Auer Verlag, in English and then Koesl/Random House in German, I understood myself as an experienced clinician, who understood the value of addressing personal and family related traumas, within a larger historical and societal context; yet also keenly aware of the practical limitations of this understanding. And then in 1997, I encountered Bert Hellinger's Systemic Constellation protocols, and afterward began to envisage ways to directly engage with collectively overwhelming events, including and beyond experiences of individuals, and families, especially in a format that could be cross-culturally viable. Over the years I have been priviledged to have engaged in many conversations with Bert Hellinger also at times together with Peter Levine, founder of the Somatic Experiencing method for understanding and resolving trauma, and my close friend and colleague for over 40 years.

Over time we turned our attention toward what might be termed those often unacknowledged "Greater Forces", shaping human and other systems; and their ongoing present and ongoing historical roles, which, with awareness, could now be made visible. Among those Greater Forces we find war, famine, immigration, emigration, religion, racism, political unrest, oppression, revolution, colonialism, poverty, class-warfare, epidemics, natural disasters, radiation and climate change. All of these and other related great and shaping forces, have many names and countless variations which manifest in both in seen and unseen dimensions. More often than not, many of these elements interact.

Underlying all of our past and ongoing collective tradgedies, we continue to find the illusion of "us and them" still at work. The first rule of ecology is that everything is related to everything else and if you can accept this basic premise then a systemic approach to understanding and resolving various levels of trauma has much to offer as a world view as well as a method. From this perspective symptoms cannot be fully understood without seeing any individual as part of a greater whole; involving their relationships, families, cultures and historical context. Even though in both field and clinical settings where it appears that we are working with just one troubled individual, we are in reality also engaging many unseen and interconnected systems which ultimately extend into a realm of some of today's most pressing and intractable social and global issues.

With the advent of the emerging field of epigenetics, it is now clear that that traumatic experiences, especially those which remain unresolved, will impact both physical and mental health; as well as ways that an individual relates to all others. The impact of unresolved traumas also includes an ability to parent and thus trauma may continue to reverberate onward through subsequent generations. To the extent that those of us engaged within the healing and helping professions are willing to become conscious of this larger reality, the more options we are able to bring toward our ongoing challenges.

Although the focus of my work has shifted toward a more systemic approach to individual and collective trauma, I am still of the view that my findings as a result of qualitative research done through the auspices of the Western Institute for Social Research have much to offer. Now, more than ever, I remain convinced that Nature continues to offer a valuable, cross-culturally available resource for understanding and resolving trauma and that our human capacity to rebound and transform traumatic experiences is innate.

Anngwyn St. Just, August 2018

INTRODUCTION

> *If you are a writer, the assimilation of important experiences almost obliges you to write about them. Writing is how you explore what it means to you, how you come to possess it, and ultimately release it.*
> Michael Crichton, Travels

I am a Somatic Traumatologist specializing in a relatively new field of Social Trauma. Trauma is defined by the American Psychiatric Asso- ciation as a response to an overwhelming life event, as defined in the Diagnostic and Statistical Manual-IV. Trauma is a process of adaptation over time. According to this definition, Post-Traumatic Stress Disorder (PTSD) is a result of complex interrelationships among psychological, biological and social factors. The key word here is "response". In individual trauma, the response is in the nervous system, not in the event.

I would agree that this definition also works well for Somatic Traumatology: An emerging field of study involved in the development of innovative methods that include psychophysiological approaches toward identifying and realigning the conscious and unconscious bodily responses to overwhelm. In the realm of Social Trauma, how- ever, I believe that we will need to expand these definitions to include the impact of unresolved trauma, not only on the individual, but upon those in relationship to traumatized people, as well as upon the larger field of local community, culture, nations, global community and Earth herself. It is important to understand, in this respect, that unresolved trauma serves to perpetuate unresolved social issues for many generations of people who may be totally unaware of these dynamics. Since I am also a cultural historian, these generational dynamics are important to me as well.

This book has been with me, in way or another, for over a decade. During this process of bringing it into form, there were two important decisions to make. The first was whether to write a volume on social trauma for mental health professionals, or to write for any and all interested readers. My second decision was to choose between a personal or professional voice. As you will see, I chose to write for any and all interested readers and from my own deeply personal perspective.

This need to write about my developing understanding of collective overwhelm has emerged from an increasing awareness that trauma and its aftermath is both endemic and epidemic throughout our world.

The psychosocial and economic impact continues to be costly. Recent research has shown that trauma victims are disproportionately likely to engage our social, medical, governmental and judicial systems. Unfortunately, in the wake of the tragic events of September nth, as our awareness of the magnitude of the issue increases, so do the limitations of the resources provided by our existing paradigms for treatment of post-traumatic stress responses. Given the increasing numbers of people identified as trauma survivors and the pressure of steadily rising health care costs; it is clear that we are moving in the direction of crisis. As the ancient Chinese proverb advises, "If we do not change directions, we are likely to wind up where we are going.

"If we are to meet our oncoming challenges we will need to expand our understanding of trauma to include the kinds of overwhelm that extend beyond a traumatized individual. The concept of social trauma or those kinds of trauma that extend beyond the individual, into the community, cultures, nations and the Earth herself is still very new. With the frequency of natural and man-made disasters, contagious diseases, wars, revolutions, ethnic cleansing, terrorism and other forms of violence increasing all over the planet, treatment is often a question of real physical, social, cultural and political survival for the involved regions.

It is now imperative for us to understand that trauma is a global issue and that there is an urgent need to develop international, cross- cultural, cost effective trauma education and recovery programs based upon easily transmitted concepts. Over and over again, in many parts of the world, it has become clear that people in disastrous situations need immediate assistance with emergency medical care, food, water and shelter. However, "one size fits all" trauma-counseling programs will never really work because people often have highly individual and culturally specific responses to overwhelming life events. Most trauma specialists experienced in the field, would agree that reactions to catastrophes vary greatly due to the nature of the incident. We must also remain aware and respectful of individual differences, as well, in age, health status, coping styles, life assumptions and previous emotional problems.

Over time, it has become increasingly clear that an understanding of trauma offers a valuable component for all of us who seek a greater understanding of the human condition. For this reason, this realm of inquiry needs to extend far beyond carefully described fields of psychiatry, psychology, sociology and even so-called psychohistory.

Over 30 years of experience in the study, treatment and teaching of trauma work, as well as graduate studies in humanities, history and art led to a perspective within which I understand and accept trauma as integral to human experience. As a historian, I have been deeply aware that the Greek verb *historien* means "to ask questions" and this has been a motivating factor in my study of trauma, as well.

Humanistic studies and attention to history, as well as to current events, reveals that the kinds of overwhelm that we experience as "traumatic" in individual, community, national and international life, have always been with us in one form or another. For *Homo sapiens,* trauma is "in the contract" so to speak, an often unavoidable component in the evolution of our understanding of ourselves, our world and the power of great and mysterious forces that shape our collective destiny. As a trauma specialist, moving beyond a focus on individual trauma into the larger realms of social trauma was a deeply personal process, for me as an individual, as a woman and also as a child of war.

Readers are invited to come along on these inquiries which constellate around three major projects undertaken while I was a graduate student at the Western Institute for Social Research in Berkeley, California. Chapters 3 through 6 are about high mountain wilderness experiences which led to a developing understanding of the power of nature as resource in healing the wounds of war. Working in the High Sierra Mountains with war trauma also led to a deeper understanding of the impact of any and all wars upon relationships, and families, that often continues to burden and disturb subsequent generations. It was here that I began to understand a need to take a closer look at war and gender issues which manifested as "Men, Women and War: And the War between Men and Women". Chapters 7 through 9 are about my next project with traumatized women at Moon Rock State Park and other locales along the Northern California coast. These chapters carry some of my gender questions into another realm of exploration involving the healing potential in work with women and nature. The Moon Rock experience, just at the edge of the Pacific Ocean, also served to expand my understanding of the cross-cultural potential of natural metaphors. Lessons learned there from my collaboration with a Brazilian shamana were to prove invaluable in preparing for the cross-cultural challenges of working with war trauma in Russia. The essential messages of the cross-cultural lessons offered by the natural world offer valuable resources for all of us working with trauma in private practice, clinics, official agencies or other settings.

Chapters10 through 13 are about my visits to Russia's only trauma clinic and their collaboration with a traditional shaman in a deep forest setting. These chapters explore our joint projects and some of the cross-cultural and gender struggles between men and women in the former Soviet Union. My time in Russia offered many insights into the ongoing generational aftermath of war, revolution and man-made disaster. Over time, having learned from all three projects, it became increasingly clear that ALL social trauma, in essence, calls for creative ways to address both individual and collective overwhelm and the need to heal broken connections. In addition, all three projects served to emphasize the importance of "relative balance" and resiliency in all levels of trauma work. It is my hope that by sharing some of these experiences that readers may become interested in possibilities for working with trauma which extend beyond the confines of medical models, state and government agencies and individual private practice. This book is an invitation to expand our thinking about trauma to include nature, shamanic wisdom, cross-cultural, non-verbal, kinesthetic methods, and an appreciation for the healing potential of community. In keeping with my choice to retain a personal voice, I have foregone any emphasis on medical, psychological or other scientific explanations of trauma. Readers in search of a handbook or a textbook will not find those resources here. Those in search of that information will find excellent references in the extensive publications of Bessel Van der Kolk and his collaborators in *Psychological Trauma* and more recently *Traumatic Stress: The Effects of Overwhelming Experience On Mind Body and Society.*

More information on the somatic approach to an understanding and treatment of trauma is available in Peter Levine's *Waking the Tiger: Healing Trauma* and in *The Body Bears the Burden: Trauma Dissociation and Disease* by Robert Scaer. I would refer those in search of self-help to Benjamin Colodzin's *How to Survive Trauma.* Gina Ross's *Beyond the Trauma Vortex: The Media's Role in Healing Fear, Terror and Violence,* carries Peter Levine's statement that "Trauma is the root of violence" into the realm of social activism.

Given the more contemplative nature of my approach as a trauma specialist and cultural historian, my piece of this unfolding collage remains with "connecting the dots", an ongoing process of exploring connections between our personal and familial destinies and the larger forces that shape human experience.

Anngwyn St. Just, January, 2006

Trauma and The Aftermath

"Turning and turning in the widening gyre The falcon cannot hear the falconer; Things fall apart;
The center cannot hold; ...
Surely some revelation is at hand."

W.B. Yeats

During the winter of 1992, I was in Moscow, visiting Valery Mikailovsky M.D., Russia's leading war trauma specialist, just after the fall of the former USSR. Valery suggested that we take some time to walk along the city's main pedestrian mall known as The Arbat. This historic avenue where Pushkin and Lenin once had their homes had become the site of a vast street market, where enthusiastic vendors were holding a bankruptcy sale of the fallen regime. They offered uniforms, jackboots, volumes on dialectical materialism and 'scientific communism'. Maps of the former Soviet Union were selling as novelties like souvenir T-shirts or Confederate flags. "As you can see," Valery offered quietly, referring to the chaos around us, "it's all falling apart. Not only here in Russia, but now we have economic collapse, war and many natural disasters all over the planet. We live in a time of rapid social change, which will also come to America.

We need new treatment models. People cannot always rely on a health care system to help them. We do not have sufficient time, money, facilities or enough people trained to do individual psychotherapy. There are so many people in need of treatment. It is important to help them find ways to help them to take as much charge of their own healing as possible."

My first trip to Russia was a shock for which I will always

be grateful. We are all, I realized, on yet another turn of a Yeat's gyre. As Leo Tolstoy knew in *The Death of Ivan Illyich,* the day-to-day life, with its patterns and familiar objects can become a husk that blocks anything innovative from coming in. Before the Industrial Revolution brought its various creature comforts, one can imagine that the shocks of winter cold, sudden poverty, plague, brutal invasions and abrupt unexplainable deaths regularly broke the Russian husk (Talbott 1992, p. 34-35). In America, the events of 9/II and our subsequent wars may be cracking our husks in ways that we may never have foreseen. While the American husk may be cracking, the container, for now, seems to be remaining somewhat intact. Nevertheless, our sense of "safety" has undergone a radical and necessary change.

"Safe" containers are of less interest to me now, especially after the events of September 11th. This planet that we live on is not particularly safe. A sense of safety is not always a realistic issue when working in the realm of global trauma. A more realistic goal may lie in the challenge of finding ways of helping people to find relative balance in an unstable world. Over time, within my clinical experience, it became increasingly clear that I needed to re-evaluate many of the premises of my medical and psychotherapeutic training. I felt that the lenses that I had been looking through were much too narrow. Individual psychotherapy in fifty-minute hours, often paid for by third-party providers, who demand access to deeply private information, offers a limited model for addressing the increasing frequency of trauma due to wars, terrorism, ecological disasters, ethnic conflicts, mass-scale rape, plague and famine happening all over the globe. Dr. Mikailovsky is quite right in his conviction that trauma is a global issue, and there is an urgent need to develop innovative local, national and international, cross-cultural, trauma education and recovery programs (Krippner and Colodzin 1989, p. 79-85; see also Colodzin 1989).

I am by nature a teacher and a clinician with little talent for organizational dynamics. What I have to offer is a perspective developed over thirty years of work with trauma in one form or another. It is important to understand that I never consciously intended to become a trauma specialist and there were many years of my adult life when I thought that I was doing something else. Over time I have come to gradually understand that my life and my work have never, ever, been separate. With hindsight, being descended from a long line of medical professionals, artists and professional military, my path toward social trauma was there long before I awoke to what it was that I was really doing.

I was born in the middle of World War II into a family that suffered heavy losses and ongoing disturbances as a result of their participation in that global conflict. As I was growing up, no one ever said much about any of that. I was well into middle age before I began to connect the dots between the experiences of war and a troubled family legacy.

My professional involvement with those suffering from encounters with the violent side of human nature, as well as the effects of "overwhelming life events" began as a student nurse in inner city Baltimore. I have a theory that what people do for a living has something to do with a need to finish the unfinished business of their parents and other members of previous generations. While I was unaware of this, at those times when I was making career choices, the impact of war upon the family and the culture has proven to be an ongoing theme in my work. Over the years, my understanding of human pain and suffering has expanded to include ways that the aftermath and lack of resolution of traumatic experiences can affect both the course and quality of individual, family, and community life.

East Baltimore, during the early sixties, had an atmosphere not unlike a war zone. Security around the teaching hospital was very tight, and the pervasive mood was of danger, sudden violence, poverty, racism and desperation. Prior to the Civil Rights movement, residues of deportation and slavery and the resentments between black and white were soon to boil over into race riots. The legacy of non-integration was taking a heavy toll. Johns Hopkins, a prestigious, well funded and internationally known teaching hospital, was an island of research and state-of-the-art excellence in health care. During my time there, as a student and emergency-room nurse, I worked together with a team of dedicated professionals who shared an urgent concern with shock and trauma on the physiological level. We were so focused on the immediate priorities of keeping people alive, that we were not aware of trauma much beyond trauma to the tissues.

In the rush of medical and surgical urgency we remained somehow disconnected from the reality that the violence and suffering that we were treating also had profound psychological and societal dimensions. The atmosphere in the emergency room was tense and intense and it became increasingly apparent to me that I was not temperamentally suited to work with what I understood to be trauma. It all seemed quite clear to me, one full moon night from "Nurse's Hell" where everything that could have gone wrong, did. Exhausted and overwhelmed, I felt an urgent need to get as far away from trauma, emergency rooms and inner city war zones as my professional life would allow.

Moving into the unraveling naiveté of my early twenties, I was convinced that, from then on, I could take absolute and complete charge of my life, which would have nothing whatsoever to do with trauma. My solution to overwhelm in the emergency room was to now immerse myself deep within the quiet and contemplative life of an art historian.

And so, I spent eight years at the University of California at Berkeley studying art, cultural history and languages. Clearly, now, in retrospect, this quiet life of research, writing and teaching had immediately and unconsciously organized itself around the themes of "trauma and the human condition."

Looking back, I now realize that my first paper in graduate school was entitled "The Impact of the Black Plague on Fourteenth Century Fresco Painting"! In retrospect, I was researching and writing about a deeply moving visual record of a medical and social trauma which devastated nearly three-fifths of the European population. This pattern continued with papers such as "Sex, Death and Disease in the Work of Edvard Munch", "Goya and the Agony of War" and more of the same.

During these studies of history, art and culture, I found myself being consistently drawn to those visual records of what I now understand as social trauma. Again, in retrospect, the direction was clear, but in my academician's mind, my life as an inner city trauma nurse and my work as an art historian remained entirely separate.

This illusion of separateness extended to include my mind and my body, as well. Years of research studies and writing had engendered an increasingly intellectual existence, with no particular attention to my physical self. Not surprisingly, over time, I was getting heavier, losing agility and often suffered constant neck pain. As my discomfort increased, someone whose counsel I trusted suggested that I get "Rolfed". I had no idea what that was, but I was in enough pain to be willing to try anything that held any promise of relief. As fate would have it, I was referred to Giovanna De Angelo, an Italian-American

Rolfer who had done her Master's degree in Fine Arts with an emphasis on sculpture. At the time, I was just completing my Master's level work in Italian Renaissance Art with an emphasis on fourteenth century sculpture. "I am still an artist," she explained, "although, now, I only sculpt people." I wanted to know how the Rolfing process worked, but questions were deferred for a later time. "For now," Giovanna advised, "the important thing is to just stay with your experience. You specialize in sculpture. Well, this is like having your portrait sculpted, with you deep inside of this work of art, which is, of course, 'you'." This language of art served as a bridge to this newly discovered realm of somatic experience. I was sufficiently intrigued, to begin a ten-session series of Rolfing sessions.

Eventually I learned that the process now known as Rolfing was developed by Ida P. Rolf, Ph. D., a biochemist trained at the College of Physicians and Surgeons at Columbia University in New York. Dr. Rolf discovered a hands-on method for rearranging soft tissue in a way that allowed the human body to rebalance itself. "For me," she said, "strength is balance. This process of moving toward bodily balance involves an order within the matrix of physical structure that expresses itself, mentally, emotionally, and spiritually, as well." Dr. Rolf's hands-on work with the connective matrix of the myofascial system proved that these tissues are pliable, sculptable, and that fascia is also an organ of communication. Her pioneering work helped to address some of the healing ingredients that were missing in my training as a nurse. Rolling emphasizes an understanding of the body, as a whole, to its parts, and to its surrounding familial, cultural and social environment.

Dr. Rolf, known to some as a "Triple Taurus form the

Bronx" was famous for her tenaciously pragmatic approach to ordering human structure. I would add that Ida P. Rolf never intended for her work become known as "Rolfing". She referred to her method as Structural Integration. As the story goes, during a stay at Esalen, before her work was widely known, Gestalt Guru Fritz Pearls used to refer his clients to "Mrs. Elbow." Around Esalen, the process was generally referred to as getting "Rolfed over", and this eventually shortened into Rolfing.

I seem to remember that sometime during the 1970's, someone referred to Rolfers as "the Marines of the consciousness movement". I had the good fortune to meet with Dr. Rolf before she died in 1979, and there was nothing New Age about this rather fierce innovator. However, there may be some truth to that rather militaristic allusion to a "special forces" perception that Rolfing offered something like a slam- dunk vehicle for rapid transformation. In my case, at least, the results were immediate and life changing. Almost immediately, the deep tissue process of Rolfing began to address the congestion in my neck. Giovanna explained that the neck, together with its structural and physiological functions, also serves as an energetic bridge between mind and body.

As long-standing tensions began to loosen, I felt waves of energy streaming throughout my entire body. I began to experience myself as a physical being, in a way that I had not been able to do since my flight from the Emergency Room. As my process of re-embodiment began, I realized that in order to manage the overwhelm in the emergency room, I had unconsciously, almost reflexively, shut down overwhelming sensations, and in so doing, had unknowingly lost a significant portion of my vitality. In response to what I now understand to be a form of secondary or vicarious traumatization, in working with shock and trauma, I had gone into a secondary shock state. From Rolfing I learned that tissues do indeed carry memories. Gradually, I began to appreciate a reality in which the body is an instrument, whose painful symptoms can serve to force us to open up into, often painful, and also liberating, new levels of consciousness.

This was the beginning of a process of connecting dots between my life as a nurse and my long years of historical studies. Fleeing the intolerable sensations of an overwhelmed emergency health professional, I retreated far away into the realm of intellect and chose to focus much of my attention around the art and cultural history of the thirteenth and fourteenth centuries. Once again, I realized that my life and work were seriously out of balance. Yet, I was beginning to develop a sense of the underlying currents of a greater wisdom at work My chosen field of specialty in cultural studies of an era had reflected on a historical and social level my own process of overwhelm and fragmentation. I realized now that seeking refuge in the isolation of my disembodied intellect, while somewhat successful, had also exacted a very high price. More importantly, however, I now understand that the 13th and 14th centuries represent a time of Renaissance in consciousness that emerged through the rediscovery of the value of an embodied life.

During my cultural and historical studies, I learned that after various inner and outer forces had overwhelmed an exhausted Greco-Roman World, wherein the center could not hold. "Turning and turning in the widening gyre ... Things fall apart; The center cannot hold; Mere anarchy is loosed upon the world ..." This image from William Butler Yeats still haunts the 21st century as powerfully as it haunted the Late Antique and Early Christian Eras. Western Civilization collapsed into centuries of disintegration and fragmentation. The end of the Classical Era was marked by fear and mystery religions that destroyed self-confidence and fostered feelings of helplessness and hopelessness.

During the so-called Dark Ages that followed, the intellectual remnants of Western culture remained alive, although scattered throughout various outposts and centers of learning. These were difficult times, and the prevailing spiritual teachings were that this world was only "a Veil of Tears" and that the deliverance of our souls could only happen in the next world, after death. The life of the body and of the senses was denigrated, as one can see through the abstracted and often still beautiful, depiction of the human form as it appears in various schools of Medieval Art. For the most part, the understanding and value of anatomy, and its potential for human inspiration, on many levels, so deeply understood by the classical world, was lost for centuries. However, it was during the early Renaissance, which literally translates as a time of 'rebirth', in the fourteenth and :fifteenth centuries that a shift in consciousness appeared which allowed the human form to emerge with anatomical accuracy. This re-embodiment of the human spirit appeared at a time when the artists and scholars began to discover lost vestiges of *studia humanitatis* central to the worldview of Antiquity.

During the Middle Ages, disembodied Western Man, had for the most part, and experienced himself as powerless and 'at the effect' of his world. The shift in perception that arrived with the Early Renaissance was made possible by the rediscovery of an understanding of anatomy which began to value the inherent power of human form. The teachings of classical texts were now appreciated in the new light of an emerging consciousness. The words of the Greek philosopher Protagoras, "Man is the measure of all things" began to fall upon fertile ground. A new, embodied and confident consciousness arose which led to the philosophy of Humanism.

Within this humanistic philosophy emerged a perception that was quite different than the Medieval belief that powerless man was at the EFFECT of his earthly world. With the new Humanism, man was perceived as CAUSE in his world, and the resulting surge of confidence led Western Civilization into a new era of optimism and forward movement which included a renewed value of the individual. The body was now a resource, rather than a liability. With hindsight, one might view this homocentric perception as arrogant. However, a wider perspective might also view the new Humanism as a necessary shift in the direction of balance. The resurgence of interest in the life of the body emerged as a central organizing principle.

It was becoming increasingly clear that years of historical studies had provided a distant mirror for my own developmental process. The personal, social and cultural collapse and fragmentation, and subsequent reorganization into a renewed sense of center and meaning were no longer separate. This sense of embodiment and renewed value of this human form was such an important organizing factor on more levels than I had ever realized.

For me, at that time, the process was quite a bit like a children's game of "Treasure Hunt", where one finds a series of envelopes that hold dues to the next step in a search. My envelope marked "embodiment" proved pivotal in my return to a sense of physical center and ground. This discovery of the power of the integration of body, mind and spirit, to move entire cultures out of fragmentation, provided a bridge to the understanding of my own process. From then on, personal and social and professional realities were no longer separate. Now, I could look forward to a shift in toward a worldview, which included a sense of confidence and a trust in the ongoing and necessary processes of upheaval and change.

And so, to the dismay of my professors, I left the study of those years from the Fall of Rome to the Early Renaissance to others. Now, in search of the wisdom of an integrated and embodied existence I began to study Rolfing. Nevertheless, I still perceived the body with a historian's eye for context. For me, as an art historian, visual depictions of the body serve, over time, as a visual record of people's understanding of themselves and their relationship to their surrounding world. In learning hands-on work with human structure, I also learned, over time, to perceive the imprints of individual, family and cultural history that dwell within human tissue.

In learning to recognize the traces of emotional history I often thought of Michelangelo and Rodin who were masters of depicting the most profound range and depth of emotional expression through the medium of human form. These artists never studied psychology, however, they were supremely gifted observers of the human condition as revealed through the body as its expressive medium. Inspired by examples from the art of the classical world, Michelangelo and Rodin brought this knowledge into the immediacy of their world through the use of live models.

In Rolfing training we practiced on each other and then worked with live models. For me it was an astonishingly different kind of educational process. Gradually, I learned to let go of my preconceived notions and enter into an interactive dialogue with many subtle layers and complexities of human form. Somewhere, toward the middle of my training, I was invited to a party for Ida Rolf. At that party I was introduced to psychologist and medical biophysicist Peter Levine, who was also a Rolfer. Quite incidentally, the meeting occurred around the time of our birthdays, and we discovered that we were both born under the astrological sign of Pisces and share the exact degree of Gemini Rising. Astrologically, this configuration indicates like-minded souls. I was intrigued with Peter's quicksilver imagery and enthusiasm for his exploration of trauma in the nervous system and also the psychological manifestations of trauma in the physical body.

That conversation with Peter in the late seventies opened a window for me to re-examine my limited notions about trauma and the inter- relationship of mind and body. My years of Rolfing practice provided an ongoing process of revelation of psychological trauma manifesting the bodies of people of all ages. Conversations with Peter continued, and I began to study Reichian and Bioenergetic work. I returned to graduate school and trained as a marriage and family therapist. While I had returned to the study of trauma, through an interest in the body mind, it was really the impact of trauma on relationships that I wan- ted to know more about. In those days, most family therapists had minimal, if any training in trauma. Conversely, most people working with trauma had little appreciation for the complexities of family and generational systems. Again, as a historian, I began to investigate and develop an understanding of the history of trauma through several generations. Over time, I learned to recognize self-replicating patterns of generational trauma. Conversations with Peter continued and we began a teaching collaboration that unfolded over the next two decades. With Peter as a scientist and me as a cultural historian the adventure continued as we observed trauma through different and entirely compatible lenses.

Peter asked me to look at a video of a two-hour session that he had done in spring of 1989. His client was a combat veteran, serving as a medic when he was wounded during the war in Vietnam. At that time we were wondering about the relationship of early childhood and other developmental traumas to overwhelming incidents in later life. While this particular session focused on resolving the aftermath of trauma, it also raised a number of questions as to the relationship between a client's unresolved issues of childhood and subsequent patterns of trauma. The issues raised here also invited an exploration of the meaning of self-similar and replicating patterns that may appear throughout the life cycle.

In the session Peter used his Somatic Experiencing technique, a body-mind approach designed to both track and alter a client's unconscious bodily responses to stress. In this way, one can create a context for re-structuring critical psychophysiological, neuromuscular and autonomic processes. Post-traumatic symptoms are used as positive resources in the healing process. In the wake of trauma, emotional and behavioral stress patterns emerge throughout the physical body. These maladaptive patterns, often deeply rooted in the autonomic nervous system and visceral organs then manifest in chronic body postures, such as immobility and submission, muscular rigidities and collapse. Peter's approach to this combat trauma session was a clear illustration of his belief that post-traumatic symptoms represent incomplete responses that will remain symptomatic until they are completed. From this perspective, post-traumatic responses represent responses that have been frozen in time. By renegotiating these responses to a traumatic episode, trauma survivors are encouraged to recall or develop those resources which were insufficient or lacking at the time of overwhelm. In completing these inner defensive responses, survivors can emerge from post-traumatic fixation and begin a movement toward a felt sense of relative balance, alertness and sense of self.

Peter referred to this therapeutic encounter as "A Developmental Approach to Combat Trauma". His client presented with what he termed "A whole string of things" and I later wrote about the session as "The Chinese Firecracker Syndrome", for reasons that it took me nearly a decade to understand.

From my perspective, the experience of Peter's client, whom I call "Jeff" who feels a "whole string of things" and patterns of trauma in his life, raises important issues regarding the nature of trauma. Although Jeff's presenting complaint of persistent neck problems clearly relate to his war injury, it soon became clear that this combat trauma could also be related to earlier events in his life. At the beginning of the session Jeff introduces himself as a 41-year-old Vietnam veteran who served as a medic during the war. While he believes that his neck problems are related to his war wounds, he also states that he feels that the war experience is related to other traumas that happened over the course of his life.

After mentioning Vietnam, Jeff talks briefly about his

early life with trauma. This conversation, held early in the session, contains all of the elements of traumatic events that were to surface during the experiential work. Jeff describes himself as an "accident" that happened after an abortion and states his belief that his lifelong feeling of distress has a physiological component. He suspects that he experienced fetal distress during gestation, inside of a "tired, tremendously stressed" mother who was an "incredibly heavy smoker".

Jeff's connection with his mother was prematurely ruptured during the eighth month of pregnancy when the placenta suddenly detached and his cesarean birth became an emergency situation. A third trauma receives brief mention. At the age of four, Jeff was molested by a neighbor boy of fifteen. When Peter suggests that Jeff focus his attention upon bodily sensations that he has been feeling near an anniversary of his Vietnam experiences, the memory that surfaces is of the much earlier trauma surrounding the sexual molestation at age four.

As Peter helps Jeff to explore and renegotiate the trauma of the molest, Jeff drops into a deeper state of overall panic as the violence of forced oral sex jammed into his small child's neck. He then experiences the panic that he felt after his parents found out about the molestation and his mother abruptly withdrew, and for reasons unknown, hemorrhaged from her mouth. This separation anxiety, in turn, evoked the earlier trauma of premature separation from his mother during the placental rupture and emergency birth. In renegotiating these separations the sobbing and shaking activates a sense of rigidity and fear in Jeff's neck.

Knowing that this is the location of a war injury, Peter directs Jeff's experience back to the battlefield. During this sequence, Jeff's experience of the combat trauma includes his realization that his feelings of being "wired and driven" and having a sense of "cold emptiness" and a "void" around his navel, "are all connected" to feelings of life-threatening separation. He was wounded in the neck, after a sudden separation from the rangers who were supposed to provide protective cover for the medics, as they went out to tend the wounded. Like his mother, Jeff suffered a violent shock and hemorrhaged from his mouth. His experience of a "whole string of things", feeling devalued, pain in the neck, oral hemorrhages and sudden separations, brought to my mind the image of a string of Chinese firecrackers with their linear arrangement of clusters of potentially combustible material. Similarly, one can picture trauma as a potentially explosive event that is also, one of many, arranged in a linear pattern along the course of a lifetime.

While I could hardly draw generalized conclusions from observing a single session, the clarity and power with which Jeff's developmental issues surfaced and clearly related to his experience of combat trauma suggest that something like a "Firecracker" phenomena might bear further investigation. If, in fact, a Firecracker Syndrome does exist, one major implication would be that the treatment strategy for trauma ' recovery should not focus only on resolving a primary traumatic episode. A more comprehensive approach to trauma recovery would then be needed in order to include the possibility that any one traumatic episode may activate others anywhere along the course of a lifetime.

A further implication would be that a treatment approach should include an understanding of the fact that not only will one trauma activate other traumas, but that ALL of these traumas are deeply interrelated.

Assisting the client in recognizing and sorting out these connections can make a significant contribution toward resolving the patterns of broken connection inherent within post-traumatic stress reactions.

At the time, I was new to the field of Traumatology and quickly learned that my "Firecracker" model presented certain legal and procedural problems for the treatment of combat trauma, in particular. While the Veteran's Administration and insurance companies may be willing to pay for the treatment of war-related episodes of trauma, they do not feel responsible for "pre-existing conditions". Nevertheless, it remained clear to me that acknowledging the interactions of several traumas with each other is essential to an understanding of psycho-physiological responses to overwhelming life events.

In the last half of the twentieth century, and now, in the dawn of our new millennium, war serves as an unwanted stimulus to further our understanding of human behavior. Whether the concern was with the nature of aggression or the healing process of the survivors, experiences at the front, in hospitals there and here at home impelled mental health professionals toward new insights.

During peace, however, the psychological lessons of war are often forgotten. The undeniably harsh reality remains, however, that war trauma impacts not only the combatants and civilians caught up in the conflagration, but all of those in relationship to those traumatized people. The generational impact of war and of war upon the family and upon relationships in general, was soon to become my next avenue of inquiry. This was not by conscious intention. Nevertheless, the Treasure Hunt continued and the "next envelope" contained a clue which led me back into my own family's history with war as well as forward into an exploration of cross-cultural options for the resolution of trauma.

Paradigm Shift

> *"I am beginning to believe that we know everything, that all history, including the history of each family, is part of us, such that, when we hear about any secret revealed, a secret about a grandfather, or an uncle, or a secret about the Battle of Dresden in 1945, our lives are made suddenly clearer to us, as the unnatural heaviness of unspoken truth is dispersed. For perhaps we are like stones; our own history and the history of this world embedded in us, we hold a sorrow deep within and cannot weep until that history is sung."*
>
> Susan Griffin, *A Chorus of Stones*

During the late 1980's the shift arrived quietly and so gradually that I didn't sense the motion. My office day began with a morning visit from Cliff Waterson, a rather intense young humanistic psychologist, new to the area, looking for like-minded colleagues. I knew that Cliff was the founder and director of his Mountain Air Institute, a non-profit public charity serving people suffering from a wide range of post-traumatic stress responses. By way of introduction Cliff offered me a copy of his self-published book. "There is nothing blatantly psychological here," he explained, "I wrote this for people who want to help themselves." On the back cover was a note that the book had been translated into Russian and several other Eastern European languages. I liked him immediately and asked him to tell me about his work.

(At "Cliff's" request I have changed his name and the names of his staff, "Nick, Singer and Carlos", as well as

"The Mountain Air Institute"). After a long silence, he began, "Private practice does not interest me. Trauma is a global issue and trauma is endemic and epidemic on this planet. Your American and European models of hourly sessions of individual psychotherapy in private offices and subsidized clinics offers limited and often inappropriate models for addressing the increasing frequency of wars, ethnic conflicts, mass-scale rape, plague and famine happening on just about every continent." Inappropriate models! I was taken aback, and I also felt that what he was saying was true and that I needed to listen. "In many parts of the world," he continued, "there is just not enough, time, money, facilities or enough trained people to focus on individual recovery work.

Do you ever think about SOCIAL TRAUMA? Do you realize that there are VAST numbers of traumatized people involved in life and death struggles with the physical, social, cultural and political survival of entire regions?" Cliff had my attention. He continued, "As awareness of the magnitude of this issue has increased, so have the limitations on the re- sources of our existing health care system. With steadily rising costs, new models are needed for cost effective, low maintenance facilities appropriate for trauma recovery." Before becoming a psychologist, I learned, Cliff had spent many years training to become a Taoist priest. He then pursued more training with Native American medicine people and remains deeply committed to a cross-cultural perspective. For years, he had perceived an ongoing need for innovative models for the treatment of trauma and was now interested in offering wilderness recovery programs for people suffering from post-traumatic stress.

At that time he was developing a high altitude wilderness base in Alpine County, halfway between Yosemite and Lake Tahoe. His camp was located near an abandoned silver mine on the site of the old ghost town of Silver City. He described his present staff as mostly comprised of combat veterans. As our conversation deepened, I learned of is interest in combat and other war-related trauma. Ideas for his wilderness program had evolved while he was serving as director of the Veteran's Administration for combat veterans suffering in the aftermath of war. Many of the veterans that his clinic attempted to serve were "Bush Vets" living in isolated wilderness areas and were distrustful of society, the Veteran's Administration, government clinics and any kind of mental health professional. Cliff began developing ways of reaching out to those alienated veterans, as well as to the "homeless" and others who had been affected by the violent side of human nature. "Wilderness," he explained, "seemed a natural place to begin, since many combat veterans instinctively feel a sense of refuge there."

Although seemingly novel, the idea of using the natural world as a resource for healing has long been a tradition in many cultures. At the time, this was all very new to me. I had spent most of my professional life as a nurse, college instructor and psychotherapist in institutional and clinical settings. Now, I realized that I was being offered an opportunity to learn and work in an entirely different environment.

Listening to Cliff, I realized how little I knew about war trauma. I was living in Europe during the 196o's and knew the social and cultural upheavals around Vietnam mostly through the foreign press. Cliff wanted to do cultural exchanges with Vietnam veterans and their

Russian counterparts who had suffered in the unpopular war in Afghanistan. As interesting as that sounded at the time, it was worlds away from the comfort of my Berkeley, California, practice.

I declined his invitation to learn more about wilderness, cross- cultural perspectives and war trauma. I carefully explained that I was totally unsuited for that kind of work, never having been camping nor ever having spent one night of my life outdoors. "You know trauma," he protested, "that's the important thing, we can train you in wilderness skills." Smiling, I thanked him again, quite sure, that, interesting as it was, his innovative approach to the healing of trauma just wasn't relevant to my life and work. On a deeper level, I also knew that I was still grieving the loss of a much-wanted child and had absolutely no energy available for exploring new directions. "Call me if you change your mind," he said, and he was gone.

Grief, grief and more grief, nevertheless provided a powerful catalyst. Later that year I returned home to the Northeast to care for my father's sister, who had suffered a stroke. Home was the 270-year- old house where many generations, including my father, had been born. Near death, my aunt suddenly remembered that there was a long-forgotten box of my father's letters, stuffed away somewhere in the back of the hall closet. This was a stunning revelation. I grew up in that rambling old house and had never known about those letters. I had only one letter from my father, written to me when I was a baby, shortly before he died in World War II. I knew that my mother had kept several smooth leather boxes of medals with ribbons attached, purple hearts for wounds, bronze and silver stars for bravery, wrapped in silk and tucked away in the bottom drawer of her bureau. All Ire- ally knew was that my father, who I did not remember, was "killed in the war." Distracted by pain, my aunt handed me her keys, and I left to find the letters.

Close to midnight I arrived at the darkened old house. Flashlight in hand, I approached my grandmother's hall closet. The narrow wedge of dark closet space was very deep, faintly smelling of mothballs and dust. Pushing aside the heavy winter coats, I knelt down and reached all the way to the back where there was indeed a cardboard carton. Slowly, I withdrew the battered box containing my father's correspondence with his mother, his grandmother and two sisters from the time that he was drafted until his death. There as well, were their letters to him, returned by the Army, each envelope marked with a large round spot drawn in black ink that indicated "deceased."

Chilled by a recent snowfall and the imminent presence of death, I built a huge fire under the arch of the massive grey-stone hearth. Tightly wrapped in long woolen afghans, carefully crocheted by my grandmother and my great-grandmother, I settled into a night of reading hundreds of fragile handwritten pages, carefully folded into tattered envelopes, now yellow and brown with age. My father's letters to his mother were upbeat and reassuring. To his two sisters, a darker picture emerged and it was to his grandmother Anna Havens that he wrote his deepest message. After receiving yet another medal for heroism, he wrote:

"I feel that I am no hero. I have done no heroic deeds and have done quite a bit of dirty work that is most un-American, according to the way that I was brought up. People slap me on the back and tell me what a swell job that I did and all the time it makes me sick in the pit of my stomach because I know that they do not know the truth ...You fight night and day and hardly remember any of it. War is like that. I used to be a sound sleeper, but no more .... memories and experience burn and I live and relive them over and over. I am pretty good at hiding my feelings and nobody would suspect my troubles but I honestly feel miserable about my part in this war. It is no glory to kill.

I love you Granny."

Vayne

"Can't sleep, experiences burn, hiding my feelings, feeling miserable about my part in this war." Combat trauma! My father was in combat, severely wounded several times, in those muddy bloody front lines for years! That short night soon passed into sunrise as the slender crescent of the waning moon faded into blue. Briefly, gently, I spoke to my aunt about the letters and thanked her for giving them to me. "Your father's death was a shock," she said, "like a grenade exploding in the midst of our family." Our family had indeed fragmented, after he died, but I never really understood why. Eventually, I learned about something which I had already unknowingly lived, without any conscious frame of reference, and that is the impact of war on relationships, upon families and that these effects continue for generations.

My aunt died in February, on the eve of Desert Storm, and was buried next to my father, together with their parents. At the funeral were friends of my father who had served with him in Italy and in France. Now in their sixties and seventies, they wore yellow ribbons in support of our troops in the Persian Gulf. They had not seen me since childhood and were startled by my resemblance to someone they had known so long ago. I asked them to tell me how he died. "In a foxhole," they said. Four of them had been pinned down for hours by a nearby German machine gun. There was no hope of escape unless someone was willing to stand up and toss a grenade that would blast the gun out of commission so that they others could run. Knowing that it would cost him his life, my father stood up and threw the grenade. I immediately flashed to my aunt's choice of words in describing the impact of my father's death. She had not known the specifics of her brother's death and still described it as "a grenade exploding in the midst of our family."

Forty-six years and two wars later this information finally arrived. Why, I wondered, was there all of this silence around such important information? My mother did not know any of this. "Who knows," she would say whenever I would ask, "whatever really happened to him?" She had nightmares for years after she remarried that my father would reappear and ask her why she did not wait.

My step-father had been part of the D-Day forces that landed in Normandy, and there again, was the silence. He never talked about his experiences, and I was slowly beginning to understand how deeply this rarely mentioned war had an ongoing impact on family life. I now knew that in order to really understand my own family dynamics war was an undeniably huge factor. I needed to know about combat and other war-related trauma. Somehow, in all of my own therapy the subject never really came up beyond the fact that my father was absent because he had died when I was a baby. I was now just beginning to learn the value of asking anyone involved in a therapeutic process, "Was anyone in your family ever involved in a war?" This question is about anyone ever involved in a war and includes those who were not combatants. Those "involved in a war" could also be civilians, spies, scientists, medical support, media, politicians and the loved ones of those who were directly or indirectly affected.

Upon returning home I immediately called Cliff Waterson and told him that I had indeed changed my mind. I told him about my father's letters and asked him to teach me all about war trauma, assuring him that I was now willing to learn any new model that would help com- bat veterans and their families. He suggested a day of walking along the coastal edges near his home adjacent to the Point Reyes National Seashore in northern California. We shared a fondness for the Marin coastline and walked for awhile, along the lengthy stretches of windy beach, without speaking. After a time, Cliff explained that he had felt somewhat burned out, "fried" and "all circuits busy" after working for years with individuals who in various ways had experienced the violence of the dark side of human nature. He left his therapeutic practice and spent two months walking through the Sierra Mountains, being quiet. Listening, feel- ing the healing powers of nature, it seemed important to find ways to bring overwhelmed people together in a setting where they had time and opportunity to heal.

Cliff described a deeply felt resonance with the plant and animal life of the mountain landscape, with a special affinity for the strength of bears and the legendary vision of eagles. Exploring the subject of animals and sharing my fondness for felines, I soon found out that Cliff did not like cats. "They do their own thing." There was a long disapproving silence as he hurled pebbles into the sea, "and they are disrespectful."

I thought, isn't it precisely those qualities that I value in the feline? Are cats truly "disrespectful?" From my perspective, they are certainly not amenable to being trained.

I have always enjoyed their unpredictability and independence. We were talking about ourselves, of course, and this seemingly casual conversation pointed directly to the course of our differences, which would unfold over time. Cliff offered me an extensive reading list and a suggested a series of films to watch, including *Razor's Edge, Platoon* and *Born of the Fourth of July.*

I agreed to attend his on-site training week in May and to complete a two-week training program in Wilderness Medicine at the Mountain Medicine Institute in Oakland, California, with special emphasis on altitude physiology.

ALPINE PERSPECTIVES

How deep our sleep last night in the mountain's heart, beneath the trees and stars, hushed by solemn sounding waterfalls. And, our first pure mountain day, warm calm, cloudless- how immeasurable it seems, how serenely wild. I can scarcely remember its beginning.

My First Summer in the Sierra by John Muir

Early in May I began training in both wilderness skills and experiential aspects of the Mountain Air post-traumatic stress recovery program. I had a week of 12-hour days learning basic technologies of camping, ranging from how to set up tents, use of a sleeping bag, gathering wood, outdoor cooking skills, water purification techniques, latrine procedures, and protecting food from animals.

I needed to learn how to plan itineraries for day trips, including alimentary supplies and transport logistics, and also to understand that these itineraries are never strict. Flexibility is a basic component of their success. I also needed to learn new first aid skills, orienteering, route finding, ridge running, snow travel, basic rock climbing and steep hillside traversing. This training also included learning how to handle various crises involving injuries, personal conflicts within groups, animal attacks, assessment of rock slide hazards, abrupt weather changes and management of hiking parties caught on peaks during lightening storms.

Staff and participants were expected to engage in all levels of camp logistics. I was greatly relieved to learn that my lack of expertise was not a major issue. There were a sufficient number of wilderness experts on staff. Cliff felt that my relative inexperience would provide encouragement for novice campers to learn along with me. "You are a terrific asset," he would often remind me, and "insecure people will realize that if inexperienced Anngwyn can do this, so can I." My comfort levels and confidence grew as I realized that participants were not expected to be extremely fit or to be expert campers, and having a wilderness novice on staff emphasized the reality that we all have different levels of skill in various areas of life and beginners are always welcome.

Cliff felt that it was crucial for all staff members, whatever their level of skill, to have a thorough experiential knowledge of the curricula. His low-key non-invasive program is based upon a belief that healing benefits derive from a combination of planned activities and non-directed individual interaction with the environment, others and self Ample time and opportunity was provided to explore whatever interests and special needs emerge from each group. Planned activities include invitations to physical challenges.

An immediate, though "invisible" physical and psychological challenge is presented by physiological adaptations required by altitude. The altitude at the Mountain Air base camp is 5000 feet, and their program takes place over a forty-square-mile area that includes five ecologically different Alpine zones, ranging in altitude from 4,500 to 9,000 feet. In my training, in addition to learning about wildlife, native plants, weather and geological patterns of each zone, I began to learn how this program uses altitude transitions between zones to create a sense of "journeying."

A sense of journeying is used to create a sense of "non-fixity" in space and time. Trauma survivors often suffer from a sense of "fixity" or feeling "stuck", in the sense that trauma has deeply disrupted a normal flow in their sense of sequence and continuity in life. Many sufferers continue to live in an emotional environment deeply bound up with a traumatic event. Often, a portion of the self remains chronically tied up or fixated on the trauma, which results in varying degrees of numbing, walling off, shutting down, dissociation and fragmentation.

Dissociative processes are often mobilized against severe distress, which may involve long-term repression of memories as well as pho- bias and other behavioral adaptations. One of the important goals in the Mountain Air program involves a process of traumatic re-integration. This can be conceptualized as a need for survivors to be able to orient themselves and their traumatic experiences in relation to past, present and future. Reconstituting the inner world of a shattered life requires not only time and an appropriate setting, but also an ability to remain in a "present oriented" state of consciousness long enough to attend to significant past events. The time, duration and meaning of a trauma and of any subsequent traumas will determine the degree of rupture or "broken connections", that is, the degree of disorganization, disorientation, and "fixity" (Lifton 1973). Fixities, or broken connections, often cause trauma survivors to suffer distortions in space and time, with staying oriented in the present as their most immediate issue. Fear of the future is often prevalent, since there is often an expectation that the past will repeat itself.

Any kind of future, then, can often only be conceptualized as a repetition of the past. This, understandably, can perpetuate anxiety and despair (Daniell 1985).

From this perspective, Cliff's Taoist orientation of a need to "move out of fixity into flow" made sense to me. His Mountain Air program gently begins to challenge traumatic "fixity" through an emphasis on activities that require bringing of one's awareness into present time. On an even subtler level, traumatic fixation is accessed through a gradual physiological stretch and rebound required in these high alti- tude environments. As the body strives toward homeostasis one is able to experience a physiological reality of challenge adaptation and self- regulation. From his studies with Native American medicine people, Cliff came to understand various ways in which altitude can provide a non-invasive intervention into the respiratory cycle which may reflect an individual organism's ability or inability to expand and contract. In a very basic sense, respiration requires the ability to take in, contain, and let go, and then again to receive, expel and give back.

There are powerful somatic metaphors residing here in both the cycles of respiration and a potential for moving out of patterns of fixity into flow. We enter this world with an inhale and leave with an exhale. In the interim, life is a long continuous series of in and out breaths. This basic physiological rhythm, essential and profound, carries the wave of life itself. Fear can be reflected in a pattern fixating the in- breath with an inability to completely relax, let go, and exhale. To fully exhale, one must be able, on some deep level, to trust that there will be an ample supply of air for a next breath and those that follow.

Collapse and defeat and depressive states can fixate in the exhale with an inability to fully "take in" the full volume of an inhalation. Higher elevations are characterized by a thinner atmosphere, and individuals ascending to levels of 7000 feet or more commonly experience symptoms as a result of hyperventilation. This subtle form of hyperventilation provides an intervention into the respiratory cycle, in which not only breathing, but all of our muscular, skeletal, visceral and soft tissue configurations involved in respiration may be locked into habitual patterns of holding. These physical patterns of restriction, or fixations, may consciously serve to hold unwanted feelings in check. If one undergoes a change of breathing patterns that require oxygenation and increased cardiac output, powerful emotions that have been held back or suppressed may then begin to surface.

As the body strives toward homeostasis, one is able to experience a physiological reality of challenge, adaptation and self-regulation. Both the conscious and unconscious experience of one's INNATE ability to restore physiological balance provides an important introduction to our inner and outer work designed to assist trauma survivors in the subsequent process of emotional re-balancing. These Alpine transition journeys include opportunities for intensive journal work using Ira J Progoff's (1975) techniques, which Cliff has found to be especially valuable for people moving through times of uncertainty and transition. Program participants are invited to use these techniques to look at the peaks and valleys of their lives, while they are moving through similar configurations in the landscape of the natural world.

These journeys also offer a series of protected pauses, during which one can deepen and expand perspective on the circumstances of one's existence. This can serve as an important tool in a process of restoring a sense of continuity and context to lives interrupted or even shattered by trauma. This method, Cliff explained, works well with a group of hikers who, while being with others, can experience a protected pause during which they can have sufficient privacy in order to delve into the salient areas of their own lives. One can work within the depths of one's own privacy while being supported in a sustaining atmosphere of the landscape and a group.

Cliff uses a specific journaling technique called "Stepping Stones", which is designed to enable participants to spontaneously reflect on significant points of movement in their lives, from the beginning to the present moment. In the wilderness one can do this while surrounded by abundant metaphors provided by the natural world of life, death, and change, as well as in a context of time expressed hourly, by season, and long traverses of geological time.

This gentle process of journaling speaks to the dissociative disintegration that characterizes the psychic numbing of a traumatic syndrome. In many cases, in order to dissociate from the intolerable pain of overwhelm, a kind of diffuse splitting occurs, and the mind is severed from its own history and its own grounding in relational forms, such as compassion for others, communal involvement and other ultimate values.

One of Cliff's favorite spots for doing "Stepping Stones," weather permitting, is to hike over Ebbett's Pass to the top of the Sierra Crest, where one can experience a feeling of being "above it all" at an altitude of 9000 feet. From there, one has a 360-degree panoramic view with a number of different perspectives from which to ponder the statement, "I was born, and then ..." Trauma survivors often have periods of amnesia space and time distortion, and difficulty staying oriented in the present time. "Stepping Stones" offers a way to make contact with elusive lines of continuity that may reveal themselves as patterns of meaning.

In my own journal, thousands of feet above the valley below, I looked down and wrote, "I was born and then ... there was WAR." My journal work during these treks helped me to realize that my decision to seek work near an abandoned silver mine in the company of combat veterans was not as strange a choice as I had originally thought. I am, of course, a daughter and step-daughter of combat veterans. However, on my mother's side, I am also descended from a long line of Cornish miners, mining engineers and amateur "rock hounds". Realizing this, I moved from an internal state of "What on earth am I doing here?" to a feeling that this work that I was learning made sense in the overall context of my life and the "unfinished business" of my generational legacy.

Metaphors available **in** this process of "Stepping Stones" are used again during a mile-long ascent up a rock-strewn creek bed to the mine site. Our principal preparation for this climb, however, is made by teaching the concepts of balance. Having already experienced the body's innate ability to re-establish balance through physiological adaptation to altitude, participants are now ready to work in more conscious ways with an understanding of balance.

Mountain Air teaches and cultivates balance as a useful strategy for anyone who is troubled by his or her own imbalances, such as passivity, conflict avoidance, and strong emotions or intrusive thoughts. This program invites one to consider that human beings are not necessarily always balanced. Ongoing balance is not a natural human condition. The task, rather, is to learn from the ways that people can lose their balance and then to gain increasing skill to rebalance.

Balance is presented as an ability to function within a particular range of energy, not too much, not too little. I learned that in exploring those areas of life experience, which can throw one out of balance, it is valuable to find ways that one can help oneself stay calm and maintain an ability to pay attention. By learning to cultivate balance, one can develop tools to use when the "fight or flight" reflex is activated.

Opportunities to apply lessons learned are provided by an experience of forging a raging, ice-cold mountain stream, which is done prior to our ascent up the mountain on our way to the mine. Cliff's program advocates using unclaimed mining sites on available public lands for wilderness experience because many of these properties are located in isolated mountainous regions, ecologically pure and rich in natural immune-enhancing qualities of clean air, clean water and freedom from noise and pollution.

In May, when I was "learning the ropes," there were two routes available for an ascent to the mine. The shortest option required crossing a stream swollen and icy with recent snow melt. This area was 30 to 40 feet across and varied in depth from two to four feet. The current was swift and very strong, and a rocky creek bed made it difficult to find stable footing. Water doesn't frighten me because I can swim, but I re- ally do not like cold. No pressure was applied for me to undertake this creek crossing. There is an alternative dry route around the water that adds about a mile and a half to a hike up to the mine and participants are given both options.

The Mountain Air program follows a respectful model of never pressuring anyone to do anything that feels frightening or overwhelming. Unlike the Outward Bound or Wilderness Challenge or Vision Quest models, Mountain Air participants are invited to have an experience of available challenges but are not encouraged to compete with themselves, each other or nature. This model that I was learning does not include deprivation, endurance or competition and does not advocate adding undue stress to an already overloaded nervous system.

While I did not relish a wade into that icy torrent, I did want to have an experiential sense of both options that participants would be offered. Carefully folding a dry change of clothing into my backpack, I decided to use a familiar approach to doing things that I didn't want to do: "Just do it quickly and get it over with." Snowflakes whizzed by my face as I followed Cliff into a racing current and tried to walk wherever he did. The immediate shock of the cold kept my attention focused on bracing my heels and staying upright. Progress was slow and somewhat steady, and I was required to adjust to limitations imposed by high water, forceful current and unstable footing. It soon became apparent that "over with quickly" was not my best option. Just past our midway point I was literally "offered a hand" which I didn't really need but was nevertheless glad to accept.

I learned that with this approach, while help is always available, it is offered sensitively and with respect. Trauma survivors often struggle with feelings of weakness and special need, along with resentment of help offered as a reminder of weakness. Not only is help often associated with weakness, but prior forms of dependency in human relationship may have proven themselves unreliable. Survivors are likely to remain on guard against promises of protection or even modest assistance. Icy currents again forced my attention to focus on only my immediate task. Life was now, suddenly in the moment, very simply all about UPRIGHT, or remaining, at least, relatively upright. And, as I had recently learned, living this life has a lot to do with a willingness to continuously lose and regain one's sense of balance.

While drying myself on the opposite bank, I remembered being told that after a period of numbness in my legs, I would experience painful stinging sensations, which would soon pass. This clear communication of information that I found to be accurate was an important step in the process of learning to trust my wilderness guides. After that my legs felt very alive, and I was very PRESENT and ready to begin an ascent to the mine site. A sense of PRESENCE is essential for a moderately difficult climb up to the mine, and this is presented as yet another opportunity for individual reflection. One is invited to both explore and to experience one's own particular resources for coping with physical limitations and discomforts as well as working through fears. An upward climb over the sunken rocks of a raveling creek bed wedged between vertical outcroppings of an unstable mountainside strewn with boulders provided ample opportunity to lose and regain one's balance. This slippery footing offered by moss-covered and unevenly graded terraces of rock served to emphasize a need for mindful attention to oneself and to the task.

This process of physiological stretch and rebound was well underway after a cold and wet experience of the stream, transitioning to the heat and dry air of a mountain slope, which rises over 1000 feet higher than the base camp below. Ultraviolet light can be dangerous at midday, so climbing expeditions are scheduled for early morning or late afternoon in order to reduce solar exposure. Safety precautions include adequate water, appropriate footwear, sunscreen, wide-brimmed hat and sunglasses.

The pacing of physically challenging activities is an important component in this model for wilderness recovery work. Hikers proceed at self-selected speeds. This decidedly non-Western approach to mountain climbing is aptly described by Robert Pirsig in *Zen and the Art of Motorcycle Maintenance:*

"Mountains should be climbed with as little effort as possible and without desire. The reality of your own nature should determine the speed. If you become restless, speed up. If you become winded, slow down. You climb mountains in equilibrium between restlessness and exhaustion. When you are no longer thinking ahead, each footstep isn't just the means to an end, but a unique event in itself THIS leaf has jagged edges. THIS rock looks loose. From THIS place the snow is less visible, even though closer. These are things you should notice anyway. To live only for some future goal is shallow. It is the sides of the mountains which sustain life, not the top ..." (Pirsig 1983, p. III}.

While wishing that I were more physically fit, a slow pace allowed ample time to enjoy the beauty of primitive lichens among the fossils and other geological variations in the rock formations. I appreciated an unhurried opportunity to enjoy plant and animal life, rich in lessons about the interdependence of all living things.

The experience of ascent is one of being surrounded by pristine natural beauty for about two-thirds of this climb. Then, quite suddenly, or so it seems, one turns a corner around a steep ravine and encounters a vast outcropping of barren land mass looming high above the creek bed. Cliff calls this area "the devastation zone". This desolate area, of granite, schist, and unstratified gravels, which covers an entire mountainside, was deeply scarred by the ravages of a silver mining boom which ran from 1868 through 1872.

A rich pinon forest and other mountain plant life was essentially torn apart and destroyed by angry Confederate soldiers who worked in the silver mines after their humiliating defeat during the Civil War. Thousands of miners cut through trees to dynamite the slopes and to tunnel through to veins of ore, which were extracted, crushed and fed to the fires of the smelting furnace. Like the veterans of Vietnam, these Confederate soldiers had to struggle to reconstruct their lives in a community eager to accumulate wealth and determined to forget the suffering and sacrifices intrinsic to an experience of war.

I now understood that this sense of historical resonance was an important factor in Cliff's choice of this particular site for working with angry war traumatized Vietnam veterans. Cliff said nothing about the history of this site. I followed him out onto a promontory overlooking the devastated mountain as late afternoon cumulus bundled together, slowly darkening the deep slate colors of the western sky. "Rest here," Cliff said, leaving for a short walk, "and then tell me about this place."

Weary from our climb, I closed my eyes and took this opportunity to deeply exhale. I slowly turned my face toward a gust of restless wind skirling off the dark mountain. Quite suddenly, my ears began to vibrate with onrushing sounds ... unbearably painful; howling waves of male rage and pain ... tears poured without understanding. Cliff returned and sat beside me, waiting.

"Do you hear that?" I asked. "Oh yes," he said, "When I found this place I heard that pain and knew that this was a place where I wanted to work." We sat in silence, and then he told me the post-war history of the mine. Then, we sat in long silence as we took in a panoramic view that surrounded and stretched beyond the proximity of this man-made devastation zone created in the aftermath of tragic human conflict.

Golden eagles circled above. For Native Americans, the thunderbird is most often depicted as an eagle. The thunderbird represents the Great Spirit who manifests storm and rain, punishment and reward. Storm and rain, beauty and ugliness. This sharp contrast between environmental beauty and wholeness and environmental ugliness is integral to the Mountain Air approach to the process of traumatic integration.

Slowly, this lesson penetrated the innermost depths of my being. Time, distance and the vast expanse of this wilderness country provides an optimal setting for shifting attention between inner and outer landscapes of beauty and ugliness in all human experience. This setting provides an opportunity to begin shifting back and forth and to practice a self-regulatory process of seeing beauty and ugliness, life and death, devastation and renewal and to be able to take in and hold all of it. The challenge then is to be willing to live within this tension of opposites with enough strength to hold a still point until the unity beyond opposites becomes manifest.

We then began our late afternoon descent through a changing landscape toward our base camp in the valley below. Recrossing that icy creek, I felt new buoyancy in my blood as we returned to camp and prepared to visit the nearby Hot Springs. Peter drove up from Reno to join us for a long soak at the end of our day. He brought a kettle of his homemade chicken soup with buffalo meatballs. "Very warming and grounding," he said, and so it was.

Mountain Air's program makes use of the natural hot springs and cold pool nearby. This "thermal detoxification" is a modification of Native American sweat-bath procedures used to cleanse, detoxify, promote deep relaxation and calm the mind. Hot mineral springs and a cold pool are also used as part of physiological stretch and rebound techniques, as well, during times of transition. Cliff feels that the natural springs are particularly effective when newly arrived participants are offered an option of "soaking out the city" in these soothing mineral baths. Over time, he learned that if we soak late in the day, it is best to end our hot-cold cycle with the cold pool. This helps body pores to contract in order to prepare for glacial mountain nights.

On our final night of the training, we built a glorious bonfire to warm us through an icy night. I sat with the others beneath the vastness of our night sky reflecting deeply on wilderness as a source of life and its creative capacities. I felt a sense of timelessness and the mysteries of existence. Silently I wondered about the role of the natural world in healing trauma. Quite suddenly our glorious fire changed. It now seemed to be transforming itself into a kinesthetic Rorschach of writing flames, weaving themselves into grotesque and ever changing blazing holographs of war, burning cities and natural disasters. Silently we stared into these twisted nightmarish forms, howling images of death, disease, deformity and destruction. No one spoke until long after the flames became embers.

During most of our time together, Cliff and I talked of his experiences with trauma and mine. In learning about war trauma I was struck by the similarities between some of the symptoms troubling combat veterans and those experienced by traumatized women that I had worked with in private practice. We noticed that trauma survivors from both groups often only felt comfortable with others who had suffered experiences similar to their own. Many of these women preferred to remain in support groups, and a number of the combat veterans felt that they could speak freely only in the safety of their late night fire circles.

We had observed that there was a measure of safety in these trauma-specific support groups, but also sensed a kind of limitation and social isolation as well. We began to wonder about the potential value of bringing these two groups together. It would be an experiment, a kind of pilot project. With no precedents to draw upon, it would be a serious stretch for both of us.

I extended an invitation to those friends, colleagues and students who I felt might be interested in participating in this "social experiment" in learning to use the natural world in healing from overwhelming life events. We managed to carry out two of those pilot projects that summer, and they provided another turning point in my work, this time in the direction of "Men, Women and War."

NIGHT JOURNEY

"We know very little about pain, and what we don't know makes it hurt all the more."
Human Options by Norman Cousins

Late in the day, as we were setting up camp, Cliff and I received word that one of our funding sources had not come through. Time for counciL We sat by the ashes of last night's bonfire. "We need money for food and supplies, ... by tomorrow, "he explained, "and I have to pay the staff up front." Half-smiling, he declared a need for "creative financing". "What's that?" I asked ..Along silence and then. "Well, do you play cards?" I answered in the negative, not comprehending the relevance of his question. "Okay then, are you psychic"? "At times," I responded, still unaware of where this conversation was headed. "Well, this needs to be one of those times," he declared. "We are going to have to drive over the pass to Nevada. There is a gambling casino there." Cliff announced that he was going to play Black Jack, and I was going to tell him whether to bid high or low. The plan was to play until we had the necessary funds and then return to base camp.

Actually the concept of "creative financing" wasn't all that foreign to me. My mother had told me more than one story of how my father's skill at poker had enabled him to send home his winnings while he was "away in the army". "Second sight runs all through my Cornish family and has been part of my Celtic roots, although it had never occurred to me to call upon it in quite this way. Coyotes howled on a distant ridge, as Cliff explained that we were leaving on a "routine errand". An unexpected snowstorm slowed our late night progress over the pass. As he carefully navigated long stretches of treacherous "white out", I asked him to tell me more about his work with war veterans.

"Do you know the Peter Gabriel song *Don't Give Up?"* As I shook my head no, he slid a cassette into his tape deck:

In this land we grew up
strong We were wanted
all along
I was taught to fight, taught to win
I never thought that I
could fail No fight left or so
it seems I am a man
whose dreams have all
deserted I've changed my
name But nobody wants
you when you lose

"For most Americans, the Vietnam War ended in April 1975," he began, "For the nine million others who were directly involved, The Vietnam Era may never be over. A lot of Vietnam vets felt blamed for losing an unwinnable war, the entire war was built on the deception that we were there to save the world from communism, the domino effect, and all that righteous rhetoric. The reality was more like a nightmare of sloshing through thigh-deep muck of mosquito-ridden rice paddies, somewhere in the midst of a long-term Vietnamese, peasant agrarian revolutionary conflict.[2]

No, muck doesn't even begin to say it. It was kind of a slithery crud, seething with leeches, jungle rot fungus, poisonous snakes and a nightmare of waterborne diseases. Those guys got ringworm, hook- worm and nasty gooksores, which eroded their flesh with large deep ulcerated circles that oozed and itched and lasted indefinitely. The heat and humidity were ongoing and unbearable. While moving through jungle slime, our troops had to wear condoms to protect them from waterborne organisms that could invade that opening and infect the liver." Cliff handed me a blanket from the back seat.

"We started chemically defoliating the jungles with a herbicide known as Agent Orange because it came in drums marked with a bright orange stripe. This defoliant was used so that the VC couldn't use the jungle for cover. However, Agent Orange contained highly toxic agents including dioxin, and a lot of our guys got poisoned. Later, some of their kids were born with horrific birth defects. For years, our government denied that there were any health problems resulting from Agent Orange." I began to understand why many Vietnam veterans have a lot of issues around betrayal.

Cliff kept talking, and I just listened. "They were out in the jungle for months at a time, with no tents, no jeeps or trucks or change of clothes, just fermenting in their own sweat and for what? This kind of unconventional warfare made no sense, even to career military. No one really understood what was going on. There were no objectives to seize and no end in sight. There was no distinction between enemy and civilians, old people and women and children were used as spies, assassins and suicide bombers. Anyone could be wired with explosives." How terrifying, I would imagine. My next question was something like, "Where could our troops turn for solace?" "Drugs," he replied, "provided some temporary comfort, but the ongoing search was for some sort of meaning, something authentic and true in the midst of these absurd hell realms of this Vietnam War."

I wanted to know more, and Cliff was willing to comply. "After the My Lai incident, in 1968, the troops were vilified as 'murderers and baby killers' ... I asked about My Lai. "The Truth is", Cliff explained, speaking very slowly now, carefully gauging my response ... "The My Lai massacre was not an isolated incident, that kind of horror happened over and over." My Lai was part of a kind of war where the VC used villages for supplies and protection. There were women, children and elderly combatants, soldiers terrorized by snipers, booby traps, punji sticks, land mines, and exhausted troops were under constant pressure to produce body counts and "Kills."

And then, "Our military propaganda dehumanized the Vietnamese as gooks and dinks ... an all around recipe for atrocity. And then, of course, there was an attempt at cover up. So, the incident came out in the media nearly two years later, after repeated denials, more lies from the government and the military and more distrust from and toward our troops ... and the anti-war movement was galvanizing."

I continued to listen while staring out into the dimly visible, frozen landscape. "Re-entry was rough, for those who made it back. Returning soldiers found no victory parades, only condemnation and apathy. Many made the transition from the rice paddies to the USA in less than 36 hours. After returning to The World, as many as 150,000 vets died from suicide, almost three times as many as died in the war. The numbers are probably higher if you include the drug and alcohol-related accidents and deaths. Those who are still around suffer from problems collectively termed 'Post-traumatic Stress Disorder'. I have never really been comfortable about that term, something like Post-traumatic Stress Response feels better, less pathologizing. In general, you could say that a lot of vets suffer from depression, alienation, isolation, anxiety, rage reactions, intrusive thoughts, difficulty with intimacy, psychic numbing, emotional devastation and self-defeating behavior."

Visibility became increasingly difficult as ice crystals continued to obscure the windshield. Progress was slow. Patiently, Cliff continued, "Cynicism and distrust is so prevalent that few seek therapeutic help of any kind." "What about VA hospitals?" I asked. "If you felt set up, lied to and betrayed and damaged by the government, would you turn to them for treatment?" "And," Cliff continued, "civilian therapists are expensive and how many of those folks have any specialized training and real expertise in combat trauma? War impacts the family, as well, as all relationships, and how many couples counselors and family therapists know or care much about war?"

"So", he continued, "a significant percentage of the homeless are combat vets, suffering from mental illness, substance abuse and drug addiction. War unleashes basic instincts, and violence, while normal in war, can also become an addiction and lands these guys in prison." Not being a vet, myself, it took me awhile, to find ways to reach out to the really alienated guys. They have so much rage, and grief and guilt. "Tell me about the guilt," I asked, remembering my father's letters.

"Guilt about things they did or didn't do in the war, but also survival guilt ... feeling like they don't deserve to be alive when other 'better' people were killed. Survival guilt is a deadly side effect of war and a major factor in many suicides ... feeling like going on with life is a kind of betrayal and the only way to balance things out is for them to join the dead. There is much more that you need to know. It is important to understand that many Vietnam veterans have issues around respect. They felt deeply disrespected in the whole process of the war, by their government, our military and by civilians at home who blamed them for losing, for war crimes, and who made no attempt to understand what they had been through. Again and again, I hear, "THEY sent us over and now THEY don't want to hear about it."

"You will find that a number of vets also have a lot of issues around language. They appreciate clear and respectful communication, after having their fill of double talk, which objectified and sanitized piles of body bags into 'acceptable losses'. These guys really do not appreciate anything that sounds like psychobabble. For them, being psychologized is experienced as objectifying and disrespectful to them as individuals. Being an individual is important to those coming out of a military experience which actively sought to eliminate any indication of critical or individual thought."

A cluster of lights appeared ahead near the casino. "Remember, please, that they consider it disrespectful to touch them without permission. Ask first, if you feel that you want to touch ... and never, ever, come toward them from behind. You could get really hurt. A lot of these guys have severe startle reaction, a reflex tactical response to any sudden change in the surroundings and can lash out suddenly, almost reflexively, if they feel threatened, or they may just suddenly hit the floor." I nodded in recognition. "Many vets are edgy, jumpy, hyper-vigilant, always on the lookout for trip wires, disturbed ground where a mine may be buried, snipers, and ambushes and escape routes. From your point of view, these guys may be over-reactive to every little thing, and that represents a failure of peacetime adaptation. Remember that a vet's point of view stems from an internal reality where survival requires a state of constant alert, ready for anything."

We entered the smoky glare of the casino shortly after midnight. Cliff explained the procedure as we quickly found a gaming table and a croupier began to deal. "Whatever you do," he cautioned, "don't think, just quiet your mind and tell me when to bid high or low." I did exactly that and within 20 minutes we had our necessary funds.

Flushed with the absolute outrageousness of our success, spirits were high, the weather had cleared and the endless potential of night sky sparkled overhead. Heading back to camp there was more Peter Gabriel ... nice and loud ...

Don't give up
We don't need much of anything
Don't give up, cause somewhere
There is a place where we
belong Rest your head, you
worry too much It's gonna be all
right When times get rough You
can fall back on us
Don't give up, please don't give up.

"How are you and Singer doing?" Cliff asked, smiling provocatively, knowing that we were still struggling. I didn't answer. "It's not just you," he explained, "Singer doesn't care much for people. He never wants to be used again and has zero confidence in authority, no trust in the system, no faith in goodness, justice or fair play. He is leery of anyone wanting to be his friend because of the way that his so-called friends acted when he got back from Nam."

Singer, a former Marine, who had been working with Cliff for years, rarely appeared without dark reflective sunglasses and his slightly disheveled jungle fatigues. Always restless, his lanky frame and hurried speech struggled to contain a potentially explosive, defensive and protective tightness. Even so, for me, he embodied a kind of sly playfulness and feral charm. With his long narrow face, and straw-colored hair tied back into a ponytail, Singer looked consider- ably younger than his forty plus a few years. "Vietnam was fought by teenagers," Cliff explained, "a lot of these guys are stuck in time, still quite young in the head."

Singer was clear that he was not fond of "therapy-type ladies" and we knew that our working relationship would take some time to smooth out. I chose to respect his distrust and to let him know that I admired his wilderness expertise, of which, I, of course, had none.

We returned to camp a few hours before sun up. Nick was waiting by the fire. In Vietnam, men learned not to sleep, or to sleep so lightly that they could rise to full alert in less than a second. The results of the constantly interrupted sleep persist indefinitely. Like so many of his comrades, Nick had forgotten how to sleep through an entire night without having to listen for the enemy. "Insomnia", he said, in a brisk matter of fact manner, "is one solution to nightmares." In contrast to Singer, Nick maintained a more conservative bearing, consciously preserving a formal military set to his shoulders and a preference for crisp khaki, and always, neutral clothing.

Nick maintained a perpetually cautious-even manner. An even gaze and handsome, unremarkable features had served him well during his tour of duty as a "spook", a field intelligence agent who held no official rank. Nick had carefully cultivated a smooth, impersonal charm which provided a seemingly agreeable smoke screen of sociability. Smiling, Cliff showed him the results of our "fund-raising expedition" and we all left to catch some sleep.

Our participants were men and women who had experienced sexual abuse, physical abuse and torture. Of the 24 participants in these two groups, women substantially outnumbered men. The women were satisfied with this ratio and, surprisingly, so were the men. In later conversations they said that they had been comfortable with the women and felt that male energy was well represented by the male staff members whose unapologetic masculinity was greatly appreciated.

The process of creating a viable container proved to be a complex and interesting project in a wilderness setting with a community of combat veterans and others suffering from various degrees of post- traumatic reactions. We set up the camp on the site of the old ghost town of Silver City, mindful that the physical boundaries and actual layout were integral to an overall plan. As holder of the feminine or "yin pole" of this project, I set up my tent up next to the kitchen, close to the fire. Cliff held the masculine "yang pole" and positioned his tent as "sentinel" at the furthest outpost of the camp, near the stony ruins of an old jailhouse. Between us, along what had been the old main street of the ghost town of Silver City, the rest of the staff had their tents. Somewhere, near the center we set up Singer' s r6-foot tipi, which we used for special councils and group sharing. This structure, I believe, created a context for trust to grow and for individual and interactional processes to deepen.

Cliff's model for group council and sharing circles is deceptively simple and grounded in mutual respect for different perceptions of reality. Everyone is asked to take responsibility for their own responses to other people and situations and not to project their feelings or their issues onto others. People are given the option to remain silent, take turns in sequence around the circle, or to speak as they feel moved in a more random "popcorn" style. It was strongly emphasized that everyone was entitled to the right to have his or her own experiences.

The initial pace of the program is very low key and relaxed. It is assumed that new arrivals may be feeling some stress from a long drive up from sea level to 5000 feet and an adjustment to camp life. People are encouraged to take their time in choosing a site and setting up their tents. While the wilderness itself serves as a powerful catalyst in healing broken connections and unfinished business from overwhelming life events, the perception of time is also an important factor in this process. The very nature of wilderness requires attention to the immediacy of survival needs. Moreover, immersion in a matrix of extremely variable temperatures, spontaneous weather patterns, while surrounded by the complexities of animal and plant life, offers ample opportunities and support for adaptation and self-regulation. Living in a wilderness environment with solar rather than "clock" time, following the rhythms of day and night cycles allowed them to access an inner rhythm and sense of flow that became synchronous with the surrounding environment. This in itself provides a context for deep healing in the areas of fragmentation and alienation.

During the initial council, participants are invited to introduce themselves, to tell why they came to the mountain program and anything else that they want us to know about themselves. We make it clear that one will ever be asked or expected to divulge anything about their trauma or abuse histories. If a group member wants to talk about their experiences, someone is always available, and painful issues can also be brought into sharing circles.

Cliff and I announced that we would be "on call" every night and that anyone needing assistance was welcome to "knock" on our tents. No one ever did. Perhaps this was because we took turns "sitting the fire circle" which meant that one of us was there until the last participant had gone to sleep. This was never announced because the intention is to create an informal opportunity for anyone to come and talk for as long as they needed without feeling that they were keeping us up. On many nights people did show up to talk if they noticed one of us sitting alone. Sitting the fire circle was a valuable counseling and deep listening experience for me. I never minded being the last one up because I was always reluctant to leave the warmth of the fire for the slippery chill of my sleeping bag.

The interactional style in the program was always open ended, very informal, and never in session format. If someone wants to talk, he or she may be invited out for a walk under the night sky, or to sit for a while by the river, or to help chop vegetables or gather firewood. Sometimes I would make "housecalls" or "tent visits" with a cup of tea for someone who was feeling lost, or frightened or was having difficulty with a decision or a problem with some other member of the group.

When one participant arrived complaining of a headache, Singer referred her to me as "Nurse Jane." This was overheard by the group and the name stuck. I didn't resist knowing that several of the veterans on staff had unpleasant experiences with mental health professionals, "really FINE people," they said, meaning "fairly incapable of normal emotion." They had much more positive associations with nurses. As the week wore on, some of the guys, who approached Nurse Jane with back pain, tick bites and digestive upsets, also wanted to talk with Anngwyn about some of the deeper issues surfacing for them.

I found that while nursing and counseling often overlap, there are also significant differences. In the trauma model that we were working with, counselors do a lot of deep listening, rather than attempting to fix, medicate, or "caretake", as nurses often do. The theory is that, in the receptivity and deep listening and careful tracking, with only an occasional intervention, one can often create a context for the participant to access his or her own resources along with those of the group and the surrounding world of nature. I found that various participants had very different ways of doing that, and that I learned much by listening and by observing the journeys of those whose lives had been profoundly affected by the dark side of the human condition.

Cliff encouraged me to scan the group for anyone who seemed out of balance, and to track them closely without appearing to do so, as this might be considered intrusive. Earlier over tea, one lady was upset to find that there were exactly the same number in our group as in her family of origin. Life at home had been deeply humiliating for her and her fears of the group were beginning to emerge. As we were leaving for the hot-springs, to "soak out the city", I asked if I could ride in her car.

On our way, she spoke about her feelings of shame that were arising in anticipating appearing before others in her bathing suit. She expressed some harsh judgments about her body and the agony of fearing that everyone's negative attention would focus on her. She said she couldn't imagine walking out to those springs without tripping and falling, dropping things and just wanting to get into a place where she could just sit down and hold onto something until she felt that she could come out and make contact. I suggested that we go for a short walk up a hill above the springs, where we could sit and observe the group soaking below. I suggested that we take an overview, so to speak. We sat for a time and I sensed how young she was feeling. I asked if she would like for me to walk out to the pool with her and she immediately said, "Yes, I really don't want to do this by myself."

Slowly, we walked out and she let go of her towel and slipped into the bubbling spring and then, in time, moved on over into the cold pool. Much later she was able to tell the others just how long that journey had seemed between those two pools. She said that while she didn't feel that she could really be in her body, she did feel that she had begun practicing "what normal could be like."

On the morning of our second day we had an orientation meeting, after breakfast in the tipi. Breakfast was available anytime from first light until around nine. Singer aroused any late sleepers with his kazoo concert or percussion piece improvised on a frying pan or soup kettle. Lunches were usually packed sometime during the morning to take along on outings. Dinner was cooked sometime before dark.

Cliff began our orientation by introducing himself and inviting his staff to do likewise. We outlined the essentials of camp safety and logistics. Staff and participants are asked to assist and participate in all aspects of camp life, but specific tasks are never assigned. Drugs and alcohol are not permitted during the program, although smoking is allowed as long as smokers respect the breathing space of non-smokers. Chocolate, coffee and sugar are abundantly available.

People were not expected to have solved all of their addiction issues before they come to work with us. Another hour or so was spent reviewing options for the kinds of activities and outings that the group could choose to do. These are variable, depending on weather, temperature and altitude. Some high altitude expeditions must be deferred until everyone has acclimatized. Ample provision is made for free time as well. People can choose to participate or not in whatever the group is doing. Sharing circles are held once a day or whenever the group feels a need.

At that first orientation, some people said only their names, and others spoke of varying concerns. One timid sounding young lady wanted us to know that she had a compulsive hand washing problem and that she did not know how she would deal with that here. She also said that she had never publicly acknowledged that compulsion.

Another woman, working in a healing and helping profession asked that no one come to her for emotional support because she just wanted to focus on her own issues. I said only that I was there to listen and to learn and that wilderness was new for me.

One woman acknowledged her fear of men and said that this embarrassed her. One of the vets came forward to say that he feels safe in the wilderness, but just going to a supermarket can sometimes feel overwhelming. Someone else, in confessing their eating disorder expressed anxiety about the "no food in tents" necessary because of the bears in this area. Cliff assured her that she was welcome to maintain whatever private food supply she wanted as long as she kept it safely locked in her car, so as not to attract animals. Another middle aged woman told us that she felt humiliated by her weight and lack of physical stamina and was afraid that she would not be able to participate in our high altitude climbs. (By carefully pacing herself, she succeeded in doing them all).

About 15 minutes into our meeting we noticed that someone was missing. The group decided to continue for another 15 minutes and if he still hadn't appeared then we would decide what to do. This was absolutely unacceptable to Singer, who announced that "someone was missing in the field" and that we needed to attend to this immediately.

While Cliff did not appear to feel that this situation warranted such urgency, he took a moment to reflect and decided to honor Singer's fear. Wilderness is fraught with hazards, and our missing person had a history of asthma. Cliff gently reminded the startled group that Singer was one of the few among us who had actually lost friends "missing in the field". We broke our circle and divided into search parties.

About an hour later our missing person was found out

on a lei- surely hike by himself He was surprised that we had noticed that he was missing and explained that he had simply "spaced out" the time and forgotten our meeting. Cliff welcomed him back into the circle, let- ting him know, without blame, that while he is with us, it is important not to go off by himself in the wilderness, and that some people had been worried and that we were all glad that he was safe.

Later in that day's sharing circle, our missing member told us that he had come to realize that, at age 7, he had been sent away from his family to an asthma clinic for more than a year. When he returned to his family, he had to work hard "to get back in" and had resented it. His experience of returning to the group now was different and that brought up considerable emotions ... "Shivers and tears," he said, and that made him feel "good to be alive."

While this disappearance had activated fear, anger and tragic memories from Vietnam for Singer, he also knew that it was his own issue and not anyone's "fault". Singer let us know that in Vietnam no one wanted to be around "frigging new guys" because FNGs didn't know the ropes and could get people killed through "spacing out". Singer popped a wad of gum and took off by himself, hiked a load of heavy equipment up the mountain and returned just in time for lunch.

Over sandwiches Cliff brought up the concept of "burbling", a term introduced into trauma recovery by a former jet pilot, now a therapist working with combat trauma. "Burble" is a military metaphor, based upon an aerodynamic principle, for a warning signal indicating the potential for overwhelming stress. Any airplane is designed to have a kind of glide curve, which determines how tightly within an arc a plane can safely fly. When an airplane is steered in a curve too tight for its aerodynamic design, it loses its ability to glide efficiently. The wings will begin to shake, and if this pressure continues to increase, will snap off, causing the plane to "crash and bum".

Mountain Air uses a number of these military metaphors as gentle and humorous ways to invite participants to learn to identify, attend to and self-regulate serious manifestations of stress phenomena.

In listening to group members informally processing our morning's "burble", I noticed how reassured people were by Cliff's response to Singer. Cliff honored Singer's fear, mobilized into action addressing not only Singer's anxiety, but also the issue of a missing person. The women in particular were reassured by this clear evidence of Singer's vulnerability and concern, even though it was very different from their own. Someone said that it was nice to be with men who weren't bulldozing their way through life, who were in pain themselves and trying to work through that pain. Another said that Singer's willingness to show his vulnerability gave her courage to share her own. Later, reflecting on the incident, a woman said that it opened her first window into allowing or accessing a connection to men. This was something that she felt that she would never be able to do because she had been so abused by males.

Later, while the women were soaking in the hot springs, the subject of Singer came up again. One of the women, whose father had been a combat veteran during World War II, noticed that Singer wore a number of medals for courage on his jacket. She remembered that her father also had medals and that they had been very important to him. She remembered her childhood as a "combat zone". She sensed a "woundedness" in Singer that she remembered in her father. Another said that she was aware that the vets on staff weren't fully recovered and that in some ways they could be "quite wild" and "not very civilized". She felt that they could be dangerous but weren't. The women seemed to be establishing a pattern of observing these men, something like anthropologists studying primates in the jungle. It was wonderful to hear them compare "field notes" as they enjoyed seeing men on a day-to-day level, just being able to watch men, just being themselves. Watching these men "in the wild", the women saw them not destroying the environment or trying to alter their surroundings. The women could choose to interact or not to interact with them, and more importantly, they noticed that these men made no attempt to control or interfere with them in any way.

This experience of men respecting something, being careful with the environment prompted one woman to realize that "maybe they would be careful with me too ... they may be trustable." She also saw how they treated the other women with patience, acceptance and respect. "Cliff is always addressing our safety, always checking in ... no cajoling, and no manipulation." This gave her courage to begin lowering her guard and feeling less defensive.

More "field notes" on the men were exchanged. "Nature is honest and men in nature are more honest and people in nature are more honest ... more real, and certainly more alive." Another woman expressed the feeling that although we could easily do an all women's wilderness recovery program, "the presence of the men freed us from having to be Amazons." Several of the women studied male staff members in contrast to their own fathers and found positive alternative models for masculine power. "The energy that is put out here is good fathering ... nurturing father, capable, protective, supportive, good teacher, allowing ... playful."

The males were well aware that they were being observed. One of the guys put it like this: "What I caught onto was a lot of the women respecting that kind of unapologetic, male presence, as something that they were afraid o but also appreciative of and so, it worked out okay." I was curious about how the men and the women felt about having me, as a woman, on our staff, and how interactions between male and female staff affected issues of safety within the group. The consensus was that there definitely needs to be one woman on staff who knows and trusts the males, to be a kind of mother or sister figure to balance all that father energy. Participants were most comfortable with a feminine presence that was "receptive" to men, but not subservient. Appreciation was expressed that both genders showed "exceptional attention to mutual boundaries", and this contributed to feelings of safety for both sexes.

"Field notes" revealed that it was primarily the males who tended our fire. Nick turned his knowledge of rock and fire toward the creation of a hearth. His sculptural talents were clearly evident in a beautifully crafted circle of stone. Nick's hearth served not only to contain the fire, but also to provide a place to sit or warm one's feet, or to set various pots and kettles used for cooking, making tea or warming dishwater.

Temperatures drop in the mountains around sundown, and people naturally gravitated to our hearth during and after dinner. Fire watching became a popular spectator event and every fire was different. A kind of sound and light display would emerge every evening. All of us watched as shapes, colors and sizes and movement patterns within the flames and embers would vary along with the density and scents that arose from the different kinds and combinations of wood.

With careful crafting and attention to spaces between logs, Nick created a series of flaming spirals and double vortices moving in intricate patterns that tunneled in and out of the fire. As people gathered to appreciate the warmth and beauty of spiraling flames, Nick withdrew into the darkness outside of our circle, visible only by the glow of his ci

In Vietnam, the dark cover of night belonged to t enemy. Night was a time of fear and firefights, ambushes and a timeless agony of boredom and waiting. Unseen enemies were nowhere and everywhere. In the jungle, every sound, any moving leaf, or breath in the dark held a threat. Aware of this, Cliff intended that evening and night times be low key and nurturing.

Sometimes we sang, told jokes, or talked or spent long hours just sitting quietly together. People remembered how scared they felt as children hearing ghost stories around a campfire. Ghost stories were rarely told around our fires, as they are not considered to be compatible with a trauma recovery curriculum designed to reduce fear. Unless a special situation demands attention, all dream-work or discussion of nightmares is done during daylight hours.

end of each week, each group spent most Ebbett's Pass, on a 9000-foot-high altitude rd the Sierra Crest. An integral part of this outing is an opportunity to do intensive journal work. As I discovered, during our May training exercises, this kind of journaling can prove highly effective in helping people to identify, process, and integrate traumatic material that may surface in conjunction with this very challenging physiological "stretch".

We gathered amongst breezes that seemed to be sweeping toward us from tall trees and surrounding woodland. Slowly, we found our way, along the borders of an ancient pine forest, bounded underfoot with a shadowy floor, rich in evidence of decay and renewal. Pine needles lay thick and springy over ungrassed slopes. Standing on carpets of brown needles and fallen leaves, we caught an occasional whiff of damp earth.

Singer led this expedition with his group of hikers that wanted to proceed at an ambitious pace. Nick and I prepared to follow with those comfortable with a moderate pace, while Cliff waited for the "Caboose" to gather. Caboose was his affectionate term for the slowest hiking group, which referred to the very last car on railway caravans. Our hikers assembled on the edge of a brightly shining, yellow green meadow, strewn with boulders and abundant patches of snow. I listened as Singer pointed to fields of com lilies just beginning to push up through dampened earth. He explained the importance of walking single file, in order to minimize damage to these emerging young flowers.

As I watched the line of people moving into a glorious spring landscape, I was deeply moved to see several abuse survivors, who had difficulty trusting men, respectfully following in Singer's combat boot footsteps. And then, for me, this peaceful scene suddenly shifted into a very different image, as I recalled being told that in Vietnam, patrols moved single file with space between each man. The first man, who was said to be "walking point", was the first to meet trip wires, land mines, booby traps and other lethal threats. The Point was often the first to be exposed to enemy fire. Walking point was an extremely dangerous job. New recruits were often assigned to walk point, in an effort to reduce the danger to experienced soldiers. These new guys were either killed, wounded or quickly learned enough to survive until there was a replacement newer than themselves. Whenever possible, it was vital to step in the exact place as the soldier in front of you.

Singer broke with usual military practice and stayed in lead position, guiding the way through the open field, single file, in order to minimize the danger to delicate alpine flora. Our afternoon seemed rich in opportunities for healing and renewal as the three groups gradually reassembled and settled down onto a slope in preparation for the "Stepping Stone" journal exercise. While they were getting comfortable and searching for their notebooks, Cliff invited them to notice the vastness of the surrounding landscape, which had the power to contain any and all of their positive and negative experiences. People took this opportunity to lengthen, stretch and mold their bodies onto the gentle sweep of an alpine upslope. The sky seemed especially high above us as we enjoyed gazing upward into a swiftly moving archipelago of clouds overhead.

"How beautiful," someone exclaimed in response to clearly visible rainbow colors and iridescent auras emanating from each cloud. "Beautiful, yes," Cliff agreed, "and unfortunately, what we are seeing is petroleum residue in our atmosphere from the burning oil wells in Kuwait .... The beauty and the devastation, here it is again." He then invited the hikers to turn their attention to our Stepping Stones. Cliff encouraged people to take their time and not to worry about completing each exercise. "Remember. We don't do these things in order to get them finished. Life is an ongoing, unfinished process."

Cliff's version of this exercise has three components:

- First, the participants are asked to imagine that they have binoculars with which they can look down from this high place onto the path of their lives and identify those negative experiences that made a difference. "I was born and then ..."
- Second, they are asked to look again along the course of their lives and identify those experiences that were nourishing. These can be major events, significant people, or simple things like a warm bath or a lovely rose. Ask yourself ... "What made a difference ...?" These nourishing experiences can help to counterbalance the negative ones in the process of bringing one's life back into balance.
- Third, people are asked to look at what choices on the journey of their lives led them to participate in this program, to be here with this group, at this point in time.

The group was invited to take a break after journaling, to stay wherever they were or to scatter to a more private place. Hiking further up the pass was also an option. For Singer's point group, this proved to be a strenuous option because the slope leading to the crest was still covered with at least two feet of melting snow. Two weeks later, when our next group arrived, this snow was almost completely gone.

Stepping Stones provided one participant who was struggling with issues of childhood incest an opportunity to realize how far she had come in her recovery work. I was tracking her closely during the ascent because I knew that she was recovering from pneumonia. She later shared her experiences of that day.

"(Cliff) led us through Stepping Stones. I was able to look over the past of my life, but the images that kept coming more clearly were the clouds, the environment and the people that I was within the moment. The haunting, being in the past trauma state, was gone.

I felt like a bubble in a line level when it reaches a balance point, a bubble nicely contained without pressure. And, the only word that kept coming was 'still point'. There was a stillness that was very comfortable. The end result was a kind of expansion. As I interpreted it, I can expand into a new experience that I did not know yet. That's how I experienced walking up to the top of the pass and looking 36o degrees around and knowing that I had made it. I felt so comfortable going at my own speed ... for me that was very strengthening. There was a great and subtle sense of accomplishment, not because I got to the top, but because I allowed myself the process of getting to the top. That is where the achievement lay. I knew that I could stop at any point; it didn't matter where I got to or how fast I got there."

Another climbed to the top and saw herself: "It was actually quite loving. Besides all the mountains and trees, I saw myself. I saw and felt the direct translation between loving self and then others. Self love and love for others flipped back and forth. It was the most free I've ever felt from judgments. The first kernel of freedom. Like being on top of a mountain and looking everywhere and loving it. Like being able to have room inside one's body that contained extremes and all of the increments in between. I can see a hillside area that had been devastated and trees that have been burned out, and I can hold that in my mind and body without experiencing sadness at their destruction or joy at all of that beauty. The feelings were in between both. This was more satisfying than being tremendously excited or tremendously joyful."

Participants had a wide variety of experiences that day: "When we did the Stepping Stones, a lot of grief came up for me. I felt like I needed to sit on a rock. I was crying and looking at the mountains all around me. Whatever was there, was there, and whatever I was feeling, the earth wasn't going to do anything about it. If I slipped and fell, a tree wasn't going to bend down and pick me up. A message came that the world isn't always a safe place and that to expect action out of something that can't perform is not entirely healthy. I began to trust that I could get some of what I need from trees and nature and that I need to look to other places for the rest. Then the rock seemed to say, 'I want your tears,' and so I moved my jacket and my tears just splashed right down onto the rock. It was very nurturing.

Everything just was, in a being state. I was there to appreciate what was all around me. Although the Earth can't physically save me, it represents something larger that can see me through the things that I need to go through in my life."

After these writing exercises, one woman found herself drawn to an edge where a rock with two flat surfaces came together to form a cradle- like seat. As she looked over an incredible vista, it occurred to her that she just wanted to scream and scream, knowing that, unlike the city, the wilderness environment can absorb it, unaffected. She felt herself expand into this possibility of having really big feelings. Having all of that room to expand served not only to allow those feelings but also to dissipate any need to actually scream. "On that edge, while I was walking up to it, it looked dangerous. But, then, I saw that it was just steep and totally manageable. Quite a metaphor for my life! I'm learning that if I am cautious and watch what I am doing, I actually can move along 'edges'; and that always staying on safe ground really limits my experience of life."

Ebett's Pass was the first time that I had taken a caboose group during an ascent and I came to understand why Cliff prefers this position. On this occasion, he had decided to remain below with those who didn't want to go any higher. Singer's party had already reached the crest and Nick was halfway up the slope, moving at the agreed upon moderate pace. The three of us in the caboose were moving slowly and stopping frequently to rest, to look around and to talk. Mostly, I listened.

One lady was moved to tears with the realization that it was truly okay for her to be wherever she was, to stop or not to stop, to do it, or not to do it, or whatever. Although climbing in the mountains was not a new experience for her, it was the :first time that she had climbed without an internal sense of pressing herself up to or beyond a limit. She found this to be very liberating and "just wonderful". It seems like such a simple thing, a very basic gesture, to allow people to have options and to support them going at their own pace. This was a very new experience for most of these trauma survivors; however, it provided a powerful catalyst in a healing process. I was continuing to learn of the profound depths possible in the apparent simplicity of this approach.

There were many occasions to observe the healing

power of very basic gestures of human kindness, which took place in the course of what seemed to be very routine interactions. The staff made every effort to remain unobtrusively attuned to needs of the participants. Someone casually mentioned that she had been freezing during the night. Cliff's offer of an extra blanket brought tears. She had grown up in a war zone where there were many other children and no extra food or blankets. She was so moved that someone had thought ahead enough to anticipate that an extra blanket might be needed.

"It was important that there was something extra and that I wasn't going to be blamed because I didn't think to bring enough for myself. I also felt that I didn't have to apologize to everybody else and give it out to them :first before I got to have it. Such a luxury, that someone else would :figure out what the others needed and would take care of it."

A strong chilling wind blew up in the late afternoon and everyone was glad to return to camp and that warmth of a :fire that Carlos had tended for us while we were gone. Carlos seldom spoke and rarely smiled. Upon our arrival, he lifted his chin the direction of fresh coffee, hot chocolate, and boiling water for tea. Laboring with stiff, tobacco stained fingers, a variety of wonderful snacks were laid out around the hearth.

A combat veteran of both World War II and Korea, Carlos's deeply set, sad brown eyes, reflected a deep experiential understanding of trauma and its aftermath. While his deteriorating health prevented him from participating in various excursions, he served in a valuable role in tending to camp security whenever we were away. The fact that he was so much older than anyone else was added an important component. The "field anthropologists" studying men had noticed that although Carlos was male, he was willing to stay behind, tend our fire and look after things. The hot drinks and abundant snacks that he prepared for the group were deeply appreciated ... as was the presence of "elder wisdom" and guardianship that allowed us to relax with some feelings of warmth safety.

Issues of safety and trust, in general, between men and women in particular, continued to surface as we began to undertake some of the more physically strenuous tasks. Crossing the icy creek was the first event in a long day of challenges that led many people into direct interaction with their traumatic material as they struggled with physical necessity of remaining in present time. One woman, whose alcoholic parents had abandoned her at an early age, did not succeed in her first attempt to cross the creek. This experience proved to be much more intense than she expected, and she quickly returned to the safety of the pebble bar. Knowing that she had an option of taking the dry route over the bridge, she nevertheless chose to take a moment, feel the ground and try again.

Silently, I offered steady eye contact as she chose to step again into the rushing water, and then I waded in behind her. Cliff waited mid-stream, ready to assist if she reached out. She did succeed this second time, feeling her legs beneath her, focused in "only now" and encouraged, she later said, by Cliff's strength and my intention, which formed a kind of "strong cord or lifeline of security". For me the lessons continued about the numerous subtle and almost invisible ways that this approach offers opportunities for positive "re-parenting". Nothing, of course, was said about re-parenting, we were simply crossing a creek on our way up to the mine.

Issues of security and trust continued to surface as we prepared to rope up an actively flowing waterfall at the top of the creek bed, near an entrance to the mine site. During one of our ascents, Cliff and Singer held the ends of the rope to guide people up and over the rock wall beneath a waterfall. "Trust" wasn't mentioned, but that certainly was the issue and everyone there had suffered deep violation and betrayals in that realm. For many the moment of truth was finding themselves hanging on to a rope in mid-air, sustained by the strength, capability and intention of Cliff on the bottom and Singer at the top. One by one, each person, in their own way, chose to negotiate this difficult passage.

Later, we received a letter from a woman who was with us that day: "Something new opened up in me that day we climbed up to the mine. I was the second one on the rope, and by then I had developed some trust in Singer. I threw my walking stick up ahead of me. The first time I missed and it fell back down. The second time I threw it and it hit Singer in the leg. And I hurt him. I know I did because I saw him wince. I felt bad, but some other part of me wondered if I wasn't trying to get a rise out of him in some way. Also, I was about to depend on him to get up that slippery incline. At first, I could not get my footing on the wet rock, so I put all of my weight on the rope. I felt him holding it. Then, I could get my own bearing on the rock. I certainly apologized to him when I got up there. He said, 'I've been hurt worse than that by a woman before.' That was a wonderful thing for him to say to me. It gave me an immediate sense that he wasn't going to turn around and hurt me because I had made such a terrible blunder."

"When I thought about it later, I could have set myself up to be hurt. In fact it didn't ruffle him very much. He never treated me like I had hurt him. It was just sort of 'one of those things'. I came down the mountain in the caboose group with him. He was so 'right there'. I found it to be incredibly healing to watch him care for people who were having a hard time."

I smiled as I read this, knowing that the slow-moving caboose was probably Singer's absolute least favorite position. Internally, I made the necessary space and time to fully appreciate how much inner work he had been willing to do in order to be willing to adjust his pace with such sensitivity. "In the Marines," I had often heard him say, "there are only two speeds, fast and dead."

Another woman also wrote to us about the importance of that day for her. "That whole day was very intense. It was so clearly a metaphor for my whole life. Walking up the stream bed to the mine, there was all this stuff loose under my feet. I didn't know where to step or to place my feet where they could be safe. I was scared that I would get hurt or that I could not get it right. Several times I looked at the ground and there would be too many choices, and if I made the wrong choice; it felt like a life-and-death situation there in front of me. At the end of the stream bed, there at the waterfall, I was just flooded with, "I can't do this, is too much." It was like sometimes get in my life: "Damn, ifs been hard enough, why do I have to do this too?" And then, to have to deal with trusting Singer! Doubting that this skinny guy was strong enough to hold me, even though I had watched him support heavier people, I was not wanting to be too heavy or too much.

I got up the waterfall. Singer didn't make fun of me. No judgments about how fat, clumsy, stupid or scared I was. He wasn't there to do any of that to me. It's like I had to have the experience before I could trust him. It was at that point that he passed the test. His words toward me and the other women were "Good!" "Great!" "Yeah, that's it!" Like he was really able to give what most of us had never experienced in our whole lives ... having a man on the other end of that rope that we trusted would not let go."

During all of our ascents to the mine, we pay careful attention to pace. With the first group, however, our pace was soon challenged by the sudden appearance of a thunderstorm rapidly blowing toward us. Ominous clouds were surrounding the devastation zone, just as our middle group was approaching the turn in the ravine where the barren land mass looms into sight. While Cliff was clearly focused on the logistics of moving people into a position of safety, his communications were calm and clear, and the group didn't get caught up in the drama of the impending storm. The woman who had expressed the most apprehension about the trip said "the rolling thunder and darkening sky felt like special effects that gave me a little push from nature to pick up my pace." This "push" felt good to her, coming from nature, rather from pushing herself or feeling pushed by others.

High mountain weather is quite unpredictable and can change rapidly. On this occasion the storm just blew around above us and then veered away toward the other side of the mountain. The journey continued onward, up to the devastation zone. Dark and rumbling clouds rendered the stark reality of devastated land mass even more immediate. We gathered along a nearby ridge which provided a clear vantage point from which to experience this vast monument to the power of unconscious destruction.

We spent most of the afternoon in this high alpine setting viewing both pristine natural beauty and devastating ugliness. The metaphor of looking at both the beauty and the devastation, within ourselves, as well as in the outer world, provides powerful material for inner and outer processing. These natural metaphors also provide opportunities for conscious awareness to begin to simultaneously hold previously separated aspects of ourselves. As one of the guys later said: "The space just started moving in on me after a period of time. I was attracted to the idea of being in a place devastated by man, in the midst of all of this beauty. I felt it move into my own experience somehow, and I could really see both the devastation and the beauty. I wouldn't normally have juxtaposed trauma that man has created on the earth with the trauma that I have experienced. It was great just being up there, surrounded by an area that's really blown up and seeing how living things can begin to grow back. But, you can still see that it was blown up ... there are scars, but it doesn't seem hopeless."

A woman with a history of drug, alcohol and sexual abuse said that she felt that her experience at the devastation zone had shifted her relationship to her trauma, in that she realized that we all have a devastation zone somewhere inside of us. The dry, scorched, scarred and wind-exposed devastation looked used and abused and reminded her of her sexuality in the wake of a nightmare of childhood violation. Seeing new vegetation struggling on the rock face was a powerful and very real image for her.

Cliff invited attention to the marvelous diversity in the shapes of junipers growing under incredibly difficult conditions. He believes that trees provide many cross-cultural metaphors important for healing and renewal. In talking about the slow-growing pinon pines, he evoked the lessons in patience, faith and nourishment that they offer. Pointing again to the junipers, he observed that except for very small areas, there is hardly enough soil, but the trees find a way to grow by planting their roots very deeply. He noted that a number of the junipers were twisted over and hugging the ground. He said that he wouldn't describe them as suffering from post-traumatic stress disorder "but rather as having adapted to their life experiences." As the group gathered to hear more, Cliff continued: "Certain things that other trees do, these trees do not do. For example, they don't stand up tall because, in their experience, that wasn't the way to let the right light in and survive. They did something else, and their lives took very interesting shapes.

As we gain more confidence that the parts of us where we know our roots lie are real and valid, it can become just :fine that we are a twisted juniper and not one of those that grew up straight. That is part of the biological diversity on this planet." In talking about the trees, Cliff provided a valuable reframing of self. concept for trauma survivors, suggesting that they not perceive them- selves as damaged people, but as creative life forms who have found ways to survive under adverse conditions.

Later in the sharing circle one woman spoke of her experience of the junipers: "When Cliff was talking, comparing trauma survivors to the twisted trees and how creatively the tree had adapted, it reminded me of how, as a trauma survivor, I always compared myself to straight trees. I thought after all my recovery that I would be a straight tree, that I would have eliminated or erased all my past history and would be a different tree. When Cliff was talking about trees that close to the ground because they get nurturing there, their nourishment, light, water and whatever else they need, they are doing the best that they can, and it hit me that it was :finally OK to not be a straight or tall tree. Not only is it OK to be a twisty tree, but this is acknowledgment that I have found a creative way to survive. The rest of life can be creatively enjoyed."

During the first week the group was small enough to meet every day in one circle, and smaller more informal groups as needed. Cliff always led the large circle and I facilitated some of the small gatherings. During the next week, our second group was too large to comfortably convene in the tipi, so whenever the entire group assembled it had to be somewhere else. Cliff decided that this format was not optimal for deep sharing and introduced the concept of "rock groups". Small round river rocks, in the same number as there were people, were divided into two groups. Half of the rocks had a white mark, and the other half didn't. People then reached into a basket to choose a rock. Then I chose a rock. If I chose a marked rock, people with marked stones came with me to the tipi. Those with plain rocks went with Cliff and had to choose another spot. If I had chosen a plain rock, those with plain rocks came with me and Cliff's group got the tipi.

We did this random selection every day. One of my rock groups subsequently became known as the "tipi meltdown". Quite by chance all of the vets were in my group that day. We agreed upon a popcorn format, in which people have the option to "pass" or not to speak. The vets did not pass. Looking around the circle and into their eyes I knew that it would not be acceptable for me to pass either. After brief words of welcome, I asked who would like to begin. One by one the vets opened up to the women their experience of the darkest aspects of the horrors of war. The specifics of those stories will remain confidential.

Together the women engaged in deep listening. As one member later described it: "I kept experiencing my mind and my body just slowly accepting things. Accepting, listening. I found that with the constant static of pain I had experienced throughout my life, it was sometimes hard to break outside of myself and listen. And, yet, I found that it was very easy in that environment. I found listening to everyone to be a very physical experience. It kept getting to my heart, opening my chest cavity. I was able to listen without having to think about my own material. The speaking of each person was so powerful that it overrode my own noise, and I experienced that as a relief in my sense of myself, that I could listen and that I had the capacity to experience and empathize with others. I had worried about that."

I listened while they listened and each person spoke. With great depth and sensitivity these men and women began to gradually uncover layers of pain arising from combat trauma, child abuse, rape and other forms of violation and its aftermath. Slowly, in fragments, somewhat like a collage, a commonality of experience began to emerge. I was astonished at how many members of this random circle had lives that were deeply affected by war. The luck of the draw resulted in the presence of abuse survivors who were children of veterans or had families affected by war in other ways. Some were currently married to veterans, siblings of veterans, or had been abused by veterans who had never sought treatment. The dominant themes that seemed to be emerging were "father" and "war". After realizing this, I decided to speak. Self-disclosure is always a risk for those in a facilitating role, but this time I decided to place my faith in authenticity.

I told them of my response to questions that arose during the journaling at Ebbett's Pass, about the life choices that had led me to decide to participate in this program at this point in time. I told them about meeting Cliff and then returning home to care for my aunt and finding my father's letters. And, I spoke about that long letter-reading night when I was trying to piece together a lifelong puzzle of who my father was and what had happened around the war. Having already met Cliff, I at least, now had a name for it and that was "combat trauma". Not only were my father's experiences deeply traumatic, but his entire family had been profoundly affected. I was still struggling to integrate all of the material that I found in that cardboard box. I was also beginning to understand that there is also such a thing as "secondary trauma" where one is traumatized by something that happens to someone else, as well as, "generational trauma" where the shock continues to impact subsequent generations.

"Why," I wondered aloud, "do so few therapists think to ask their clients, 'Was anyone in your family or your life ever in a war?' How many civilian therapists really understand anything about the complexities of war? Why do we persist in believing that only those in combat are at risk for war trauma? How much do we understand about the impact of war upon relationships or the capacity for intimacy? What about the relationship between war trauma and substance abuse, ad- diction, boundary violations and sexual trauma? In what ways does war influence the way that we parent? What is the correlation with domestic violence?" Finally, I just let my questions rest.

In the fall of that year, Cliff invited a delegation of Russian war trauma specialists and a group of veterans from the Russian war in Afghanistan to visit. These Russians were very interested in what we were doing in the mountains and in the ways that we were using the natural world in the treatment of trauma and war trauma, in particular. At that time, Russia had little money for costly treatment centers or psychotropic medications. The medical model of psychotherapy treatment in individual sessions is a Western concept and definitely not the Russian way. In Russia land is plentiful and the people have the deepest respect for the healing powers of nature.

The Russian delegation was headed by Valery Mikhailovich Mikhailovsky M. D., founder and director of Russia's only war trauma clinic, located in Zelenograd, just outside of Moscow. During the course of his visit we discovered that we shared a deep concern for the generational and societal factors that contribute to the ongoing cycles of trauma. Both of us had family members in World War I and IL Initially, Dr. Mikailovsky did not understand why we felt that it was important to include women in war trauma recovery programs. "In Russia," he said, "war is men's business". "I wonder," I said, "if your mother and grandmother would agree with that, and how about your wife, your sister and your daughter?" "What about the women who were mothers, wives, siblings, medical, logistical and technical support, spies and civilians during the wars?" Valery acknowledged that the Russian war recovery programs did not include women. He further went on to say that they did not have any programs specifically designed to address the needs of traumatized women. He then asked if I would be willing to come to Russia to work together with his staff to create a program especially designed to address the needs of traumatized women. Even more specifically, he wanted the program to include experiences with the natural world.

I accepted Valery's generous invitation and it was nearly a year before we could make the necessary arrangements. Meanwhile, I realized that had much to learn about the specifics of using the natural world in healing the wounded feminine. In discussing these new directions, Cliff was very clear. In a rare moment of physical contact, Cliff took me by my shoulders "You need to go now, form your own organization and keep moving to bring the awareness of social trauma into ever widening spheres. I need to stay here in the mountains with my friends". "No!" I protested, "Yes," he said, with a knowing grin, pointing upward to the meteor shower cascading overhead. Reflecting back on my experiences with Cliff's program, it seems that, theoretically, at least, many of the healing experiences could be replicated in a residential environment with ample opportunities to interact with other group members. In this respect many of the elements of the program such as deep listening, respectful communication, journaling and cultivating balance could be adapted to a non-wilderness environment The ability to create a relatively safe container and address the issues of trust does not require a wilderness setting.

Nevertheless, in my experience the use of natural metaphors in a wilderness environment proved highly effective in helping trauma survivors to shift their relationship to overwhelming life events. The life cycle of trees, for example, offers important lessons in adaptation, renewal and creative use of resources. Experiences offered in and around the devastation zone also served as a statement of hope, affirming the possibility that people and landscape can heal together. In this respect, in particular, choice of setting is especially conducive to traumatic re-integration.

The stark contrast between environmental beauty and wholeness and environmental ugliness was an extremely important element in the success of Cliff's approach to the process of traumatic integration. Time, distance and a vast expanse of wilderness country provide optimal settings for shifting attention between inner and outer landscapes of beauty and ugliness in all human experience. The nature of the setting provides ample opportunities to begin shifting back and forth and to practice the self-regulatory process of seeing both and ugliness, life and death, devastation and renewal. Cliff's model also recognizes that the value of being together with others in the natural world is part of the healing process. From this perspective it is definitely intended that reconnecting with the "unbroken web of wholeness" included one's fellow human beings. This is a vital component to any trauma recovery program which must recognize how devastating the feelings of grief, rage and outrage that often occur in the aftermath of trauma, can be to the quality of human relationships.

Residential programs that address the issues of post-traumatic stress can be very expensive to establish and maintain. Given the limitations on the resources provided by our existing health care system, wilderness recovery programs using public lands offer cost-effective, low maintenance options worth serious consideration.

Options, I believe, are important in these rapidly changing, perilous times. In thinking about wilderness as a therapeutic tool in healing of post-traumatic responses I recalled R. J. Lifton's discussion in his book, *The Broken Connection,* of the importance of nature for the survivors of Hiroshima. While struggling to re-establish their own sense of continuity, the Hiroshima survivors often quoted the ancient Japanese (originally Chinese) saying, "The state may collapse, but the mountains and rivers remain." Immediately after the bomb fell, the most terrifying rumor that swept through the population was that trees, grass and flowers would never grow again in Hiroshima. The subsequent appearance of early spring buds symbolized "a new feeling of relief and hope."

WOMEN ON THE MOON

No one ever told us that we had to study our lives, make of our lives a study, as if/earning natural history ...

from *"Transcendental Etude"* in *The Dream of a Common Language* by Adrienne Rich

During the time that I was working in a high Alpine setting with both men and women who had suffered overwhelming life events, I ob- served and listened to the ways that women found to use the natural world in their own process of healing. I wondered if and how it might be different if women were given an opportunity to do that in a very different setting with an all female staff. In wondering about women and their intuitive relationship to the natural world I thought that it would be interesting to choose a retreat site that had many elements strongly evocative of the feminine.

I decided to invite various women from the healing arts and helping professions to join us in exploring the possibilities for women to find their own ways of healing and renewal. In addition, I asked my Russian language tutor to come along and work with me in developing vocabulary for my forthcoming work with women in Valery's clinic in Zelenograd. I also decided to invite Brazilian shamana Maria Lucia Saur Holloman to serve as teacher, "technician of the sacred", and guide during our quest for experiential knowledge of woman and nature.
Maria and I shared a mutual friend and colleague in Peter Levine, and I had several opportunities to observe her working alongside him in the renegotiations of

overwhelming life experiences. I was deeply curious about her perceptions as to the ways in which the spirit realm can interact with both psychotherapy and body work during the healing process. The word shaman is derived from the Russian *shaman.* Weston Le Barre, a distinguished professor of anthropology at Duke University, notes that the shaman is the world's oldest professional and personage from which both modem physician and priest descend.

"The shaman was the original artist, dancer, musician, singer, dramatist, intellectual, poet, bard, ambassador, advisor of chiefs and kings, entertainer, actor, clown, stage magician, juggler, folksinger, weather- man, artisan, hero and trickster/transformer" (Achterberg,1985). Several scholars feel that the true roots of shamanism in Western civilization lie in the practices of wise women who were considered to be ultimate purveyors of the supernatural and hence of the imagination. The work of the shaman is conducted in the realm of the imagination, and their expertise in using that terrain for the benefit of the community has been recognized throughout recorded history. This oldest and most widespread method of healing with the imagination heals "broken connections" by restoring a sense of contact with an unbroken web of wholeness. In the realm of a shaman, everything is interrelated and nothing exists in isolation. In a time when Western thought finds itself in a crisis situation in dealing with a seriously imperiled planet, shamanic teachings about the unity of all things and all beings may have a healing role to play.

In seeking to create a context for healing for women, I remember an old Chinese story which evokes the spirit of feminine consciousness. In this story, a remote village was stricken with drought, their harvest was threatened, and the people were faced with starvation. In desperation, they sent for a Rainmaker. Eventually, a little old man arrived and the villagers asked him what he needed in order to perform his magic. "Nothing," he replied, "except a quiet room where I may be alone."

He lived there quietly for two days, and on the third day it rained. The magic of this Rainmaker was in his capacity to *allow* things to happen, rather than attempt to cause them. The villagers had frantically tried to *make* the rain come. The Rainmaker, however, simply created space for rain to fall. Because he willed nothing and asked nothing, he exerted a very different influence from the deliberate, organizing principle of the masculine. By his example, the Rainmaker revealed that some things just have to be allowed to happen. These are those things we cannot order and control. For them, we simply have to wait and allow them the possibility of being. The central concept of Taoism was expressed through a character which means "by itself so" and is sometimes translated as "spontaneity" (Colegrave 1979). And so the concept of "contemplative camping" emerged. I wanted to find a way for women to be together in the natural world as part of a low key, non-invasive format, designed to promote a sense of confidence and well being. I also wanted to evoke a power from within, without provocation, confrontation or direct challenge.

In conference with a group of women friends, we settled on a coastal site a few miles south of Gualala known as "Moon Rock". This surreal stretch of barren rocks and cliffs had many "lunar" elements strongly evocative of the ancient archetypal feminine. We found numerous water caves, along with sensuous swelling undulant forms, abundant in the sandstone landscape formed sometime in the volcanic twilight of prehistoric time.

We set up our base camp at Gerstle Cove, at a state park site near Salt Point Marine Preserve, about a 15-

minute hike from Moon Rock. Our campground area spread over a gentle hillside slope, densely forested on the north and opening west toward a rocky meadow that overlooked the Pacific Ocean. We chose a sheltered area that faced an open field, south of the camping area, as a place to set up our yurt.

This 16 foot round tent served as a primary space for council and group sharing. The circular form of the yurt appealed to us since the circle has emerged as an important symbol in women's art; as a principal image of an impulse toward wholeness in women's culture. The yurt had practical appeal, as well, since the task of transporting the canvas and the frame and setting it up was considerably more manage- able than dealing with the long poles required for a tipi. Another practical concern was for our women's safety. This was of particular concern, since several of our participants had been brutally raped. One side of our campsite was situated on a protected edge on the park site, with rangers available if we needed them. Another edge opened out toward the nurturing matrix of ocean wilderness – so intrinsically vital to health and well-being – and to maintaining the balance of our planetary biosphere.

The ocean influences broad cycles of climate and weather. It absorbs most of the sunlight that strikes the earth and creates most of the oxygen that we breathe. The ocean absorbs huge quantities of carbon dioxide and serves as a source of most fresh water. Also important is the fact that the sea merges with the atmosphere and both join the land as a single dynamic system.

For most of the women the ocean proved to be the most evocative element at our retreat site. Several women offered the following: "Some of the Native Americans call it Grandmother Ocean. She is feminine, a big dark deep

Feminine. Whenever I am trying to shoulder too much, I give my problems away to the power of the ocean. I think that the ocean, with its rhythms and its power, can teach you to give your weight to something bigger ... and more powerful than you are. Seeing the power of the ocean, I know that I can never really control or hold on to anything or anyone. Being with the ocean, the rhythmical breathing of the waves, the water and the lapping sounds is like being with the tidal rhythms of the womb."

And in a similar vein: "I see the ocean; the curl of the wave as it comes in and then suddenly rolls out. It's like a massive surge of energy that comes, makes itself available and then removes itself and then does this over and over. Being exposed to that rhythm, at any stage of your life, you can learn how to move in and join it, and out again without getting hit or smashed.

I think it teaches a profound philosophy of 'what is given to you is also taken away.' A rhythm, a continuing cycle, an ongoing flow is the only certainty."

The vastness of the sea was perceived as a powerful healing re- source. "The ocean gives us so much space to just grieve and let go, any way that you need to let go and the sea is big enough to take it. If you are feeling just bitter, just filthy, bitchy, terrible and you can yell and scream and spit and seethe into it and it can absorb that and bring you back into a place of beauty. It's just amazing how much it can take and still offer beauty."

For one woman who lived in a pastoral area near the coast, the ocean around Moon Rock brought up feelings of danger and human fragility. "The ocean there had a much more dangerous feeling, of a more elemental meeting of myself and of nature at the edge of the ocean. I felt the force of the ocean and the fragility of the human body, how fragile we are compared to those rocks, and how quickly our time span is in comparison to the ocean and the rocks. So there was a feeling of being on the edge ... a metaphor for just walking that fine line that we all walk between being alive and being dead."

The ocean also brought up other kinds of fear, such as fear of the power of The Feminine: "For me, the ocean was a feminine place of power for women, but it can also stimulate a lot of fear. There is the very real physical fear of the feminine manifested outside of the self ... and then reflected back to us. We haven't been taught to contain our own power without being overwhelmed by it and I think that it can scare us and that this is also the reason for some of the backlash against the feminine."

Overall, we were quite content with this powerful coastal site, rich in "edges" with its juxtaposition of safety and wilderness, land and water. Cultural historian William Irwin Thompson helps to remind us that we are all on an edge and nothing helps perception like an edge. "Edges," he says, "are places where familiar things end and something else" begins. Edges are important because they define limitations in order to deliver us from them" (Thompson 1971).

And so, we set up our particular edge at Gerstle Cove, where elements meet along this interface of sea and shore, where time and eternity splatter each other with foam. In the intermingling realms of unconscious and conscious, civilization and nature, we sensed a conducive place to explore the process of healing and transformation. In my previous work with groups seeking healing experiences in the natural world, I gained an increasing appreciation of the role of the perception of time in lowering participants' levels of stress. Most agreed that there was a very different sense of time out in the wilderness. Most also felt that time slowed down and expanded. A significant feature of this slowing and expansion seemed to be a more organic time frame that was oriented to solar rather than to clock time. The perception of many is reflected in responses to my questions about the experience of time in the natural world.

"Yes, I was able to tune in, by not looking at my watch and living according to the sun and stars. Living by the day and night cycle as opposed to the hourly cycle. Whenever I look at a clock I am out of my experienced, internal flow of what's going on NOW."

This perception was echoed by others in very similar language: "Living our whole being. The day and night cycles are very important. In the wilderness, I let go of ordinary ways of thinking of time. I didn't have a watch. I found myself following the sun a lot, just moving with my own rhythms ... I let go of controlling time." And again:

"Time just kind of disappeared. I felt like I had been there for months and it was wonderful. Very different from my daily life at home which is tightly organized and scheduled.... there was light time and dark time. Morning and evening all blended together." One person simply stated, "... time slowed down. Time was a lot nicer."

With this information in mind and a perception that many over-functioning women "trying to do it all" might be tyrannized by time, the curriculum was designed to run on organic rather than clock time. This shift from *chronos* to *kairos* meant that we got up sometime after dawn and went to sleep sometime after dark. Activities lasted as long as they did or didn't and then we would or wouldn't do something else. Group participation and all activities, except the initial orientation, was optional.

This four-day gathering was scheduled to begin on a Thursday afternoon, sometime after lunch. The support staff arrived the day before to prepare the site, set up our yurt and organize food logistics. Much of the meal preparation had been done in advance with an emphasis on options.

Our menu included two warm cooked meals a day, with sandwiches, salads and fruit for lunch. Each meal offered a vegetarian entree and was mindful of women's concerns for health and excess calories. Healthful snacks were offered in abundance, and there was always plenty of coffee, teas, chocolate and cookies. Maria and I arrived Thursday in time to help set up the yurt. The women had been asked to bring blankets, cushions, rugs, animal skins or whatever, to spread around the tent floor to provide additional warmth and comfort. Having a fire inside would not have been safe out in the midst of a dry meadow. We began spreading warm things around the interior space and then creating a focal point of warmth and light. One of the women arranged a large collection of candles of various size shapes and colors on a circular metal tray. She then placed the tray in the center of our floor-space, directly below a circular opening in the roof of the tent.

Someone had found an interesting branch of very old wood and it was decided that this would serve as the "talking stick" during group sharing. This custom derives from several indigenous cultures as a clear means of indicating who "has the floor" during group discussions. We added a few strands of silvery moss and placed our stick near our central tray. Later, several participants further embellished the wood with tiny cerulean jay feathers, abalone shards and other found treasures.

Maria headed off toward the "kitchen" for supplies. Eventually, she found a large metal mixing bowl and began boiling water to prepare an infusion of fresh jasmine. "Jasmine," she said, "is wonderful for diffusing negativity." Slowly wandering through my garden she had gathered armfuls of long slender vines covered with lacy clusters of fragrant, white, star-shaped blossoms and gently folded them into a bag to bring for our retreat. "It is important," she cautioned, while arranging the vines into the bowl, "to not overheat these flowers. Never boil them in water. You add boiling water to a bowl. This brings just enough heat to release the power of their fragrance." When her infusion was ready, she set it down, just inside the entrance to the yurt.

At our first gathering we began to address the purpose of this retreat, which was to learn as much as we could from ourselves, and each other, about how women can use resources of the natural world to heal, or at least manage, overwhelming life events. While I came primarily to learn, I anticipated that this process would entail at least some teaching on my part. An educator schooled entirely in Western traditions, I had learned that one teaches by imparting information. Maria was schooled in an entirely different tradition, and her ways of giving and receiving information were very different from mine. This difference was apparent from the outset. Her shamanic teaching style is often very indirect and done through gentle humor and reflection. She likes to embody an issue and then model options for resolution.

Maria began with a question. "So, I have come all the way from Brazil to be with you. Now, what would you like me to do?" Her question was received in silence. How could it be that this shamana who is here to lead the retreat doesn't know what to do? The teaching has begun, and I follow her lead. "You don't need to do anything Maria," I tell her. "Just be yourself. And then, tell us what you want to do." "Just be myself? You really mean that?" "Yes," I said quietly. "I really mean that."

Maria responded with a radiant smile. "Well, who I am is one very tired woman! Like all of you, I work, I have a family and I give a lot to those who need it, and maybe to those who don't. And, what I want to do is go to my tent and take a nap!" "Good," I said, "please feel free to rest whenever you need to." Maria then asked, "Is anyone else tired?" A wave of recognition swept through the circle. A deep unspoken issue had been identified and addressed. While it was true that Maria was tired, as was I, the issue was much larger. Women are tired and reluctant to rest when they need to. Permission was given for women to acknowledge their exhaustion and to rest. Maria walked her talk and went straight to her tent for a nap. At least half of the group decided to do likewise. One of the women spoke for others, as well, when she found feelings of guilt welling up around the need to rest.

"Maria's nap astonished me. I don't think women needing to rest is really sanctioned. I feel like there is a judgment from the culture and from ourselves about resting. My guess is that women are the ones who are supposed to hold the world together and resting is like relinquishing responsibility. In my household it was not 0K to rest. I had to always be doing something or I was in big trouble. To be caught resting was like 'How dare you not be holding it together?' When I rest I feel as though I am being terribly lazy, but I love it all the same!"

Several participants decided to rest for the remainder of our afternoon. The others chose to join us for a walk along Shell Beach. We found our way through thick groves of cypress and eucalyptus, out onto a meadow path surrounded by tall grasses and abundant wildflowers. Gentle breezes smelling of anise and a faint fishy rankness grew stronger as we approached the shoreline. Sea birds swirled above strong currents and churning waves. This particular stretch of northern California coast is visually rich in sea- sculpted rocky formations, which have been worn and battered into fissures, caves and arches. Ceaseless carving of wind and water has created a variety of habitats suited to life forms designed to tolerate seasonal trials and harsh conditions. We spent the rest of an afternoon wandering along this narrow strip of intertidal region; an area of rock and damp sand bounded by an ongoing flow of high and low tides. Here, diverse environments of land and sea meet and meld. Together, we slowly and carefully explored this edge.

Our walk continued amongst a complex variety of organisms destined to dwell within the confines of shallow tidal pool, all of them desperately competing for survival within a severely limited space. Something familiar here resonates with our current situation of over- population and uncertain ecological changes. In several of us, our walk also evokes a deep resonance and a longing for an understanding of origins. Our origins may lie somewhere within in this element; rich, tidal ooze, shallow reflections of reflexive motility and spontaneous nerve endings waving through delicate strands of seaweed and fine powdered sand, or maybe not.

While human primates arrived only a couple of million years ago, *homo sapiens* carries a range of sensitivity as vast as our life spawning seas. We may never fully detach from these notions of our oceanic origins. Our wandering women soon encountered a number of our fellow mammals. It was just past mid-summer and many mother seals could be seen, together with their pups, sunning themselves along a myriad of rocky inlets.

The scientific name for seals and sea lions is *Pinniped,* which literally means, "feathered feet". This species, it seems, made some interesting evolutionary choices. Fossil evidence reveals that their short, heat-conserving flippers that serve as paddles for both steering and propulsion evolved from terrestrial limbs. Although they once lived on land, sea lions, along with whales, dolphins and walruses returned to the sea. They now remain only partially bound to the shore where they sun, sleep, mate and bear their young. Turning my attention from these seals to the women walking along the sand, I was suddenly curious about the uprightness of their female forms.

Poet Martha Heyneman (1985) reminds us that upright posture is the first peculiarly human characteristic to appear in the fossil record. This evolutionary leap must have involved enormous effort, requiring extensive redistribution of muscle and realignment of bone. While this new posture did free our hands, whatever survival value it could have had in and of itself is not readily apparent, especially for females. An upright stance required that soft breasts and vulnerable bellies would be carried out in front exposed to every shock and blow. Nevertheless, all of these evolutionary struggles, along with the blind, forgotten struggles of gestation and infancy have brought the body upright. What, I wonder, has uprightness to do with our changing understanding of the universe is, what is possible for us, and how ought we to live together on this planet?

Did human consciousness grow up slowly from below like a plant reaching up for light? Or did it flash down upon us like a lightning bolt of revelation? Remaining effortlessly upright in earth's gravitational field does serve to create a sensation of polarity of an above and a below and also a back and front. Is this awareness of our physical orientation an important component in human evolution? And, how does this relate to gender?

Ida Rolf believed that awareness of our physical

orientation is an important component of human evolution. Dr. Rolf taught that physical balance and awareness enhance the ability to keep inner and outer worlds in balance and that this, in turn, increases our capacity to remain fully present in present time. These teachings remain as essential components of her Structural Integration training. My years of practicing Rolfing, along with Reichian and Bioenergetic methods and oriental martial arts techniques, all served to emphasize the importance of orienting and grounding.

Grounding is generally understood to be an energetic reality in which an individual experiences a felt sense of connection with ground and the gravitational forces of our earth. Having one's "feet on the ground" is body language for being stable and "in touch" with reality and not operating out of any illusions, conscious or unconscious.

In a literal sense, most people do have their feet on the ground. In an energetic sense, however, this is often not the case. If a person's energy does not flow strongly into his or her feet, then feeling contact with the earth will be very limited. The orientation and grounding exercises that I have been taught were done in a standing position and were the same for both genders. In observing women in our natural world, I began to suspect that female grounding patterns are different than those of males. However, it was not until I began to develop the cross-cultural work in Russia, that these gender differences became dear.

Curiosity had led Maria and the others further along the shoreline, and just beyond a sheltered cove, they had made a discovery. They waved and signaled us upward along a steep path that emerged on top of a rocky cliff where within a few steps we found ourselves on the edge of an enormous sea cavern. Looking down into this cave we saw emerald green mosses and delicate ferns on a shady side of the interior revealing the presence of a freshwater spring that trickled gently down rough hewn rock face into salt-water currents below. We were fascinated by variegated patterns of light and shadow that played across moist rocky surfaces refracting down into these churning waters of unknown depth.

The women perceived this cave as enormously feminine. "The Dark Feminine", someone said. "Mother Earth" and "uterine" were terms that arose as the group contemplated their discovery. We were mesmerized by sounds of gentle rhythmic splashes with echoes and roaring that reverberated at irregular intervals, as a surging tide hurled wave after wave against cavernous walls. There was something deeply primal, and primeval, about this place that the group had identified as Feminine.

This perception was not surprising because cave imagery has long been associated with various aspects an archetypal feminine as well as with rites of sacred passage. In many cultures, caves represent inner esoteric knowledge, and hidden wisdom. Caves are secret, often sacred places of initiation, burial, ceremonial rebirth and mystery. Their entrances may be hidden by labyrinths or accessible only by dangerous pathways. As such, they are often chosen as sites of rites of passage. A cave is also the womb of Mother Earth in her sheltering aspect.

As a participant observer, I sat down to observe how these women might use this site for healing. Without explanation, Maria stretched herself out, facing downward on a rock ledge with her head oriented toward the rim of the cave. Several women did likewise and I decided to try it.

Lying on my belly near the top of the cave my soft mammalian body could feel churning surf vibrating upward through multiple layers of rock. Settling into those vibrations and a number of other rhythmic sounds below felt strangely familiar and deeply soothing. Womblike. Connected.

"Rocks," Maria said, "are very ancient beings. They have been on Earth for so long that they have much to teach us. So, what I am doing is just lying here, slowing down and being receptive ... just being with them. Rock messages don't come in thought form. They come into my body as softening up. Opening up. Not having to push myself so hard. Because they are rocks and they have been here so long, they don't have to do much. They don't have to move much. They are prints, encoded records of what has been going on here on Earth for eons. They have felt it all and everything is recorded in them."

Lying there at this cave opening, I was grounded more completely than I could have been standing. "Grounding," Ida Rolf said, "comes from connection to the mother. And, those who didn't get it from their mothers can still get it from The Mother" (Feitis 1978).

This was very good, I thought. Everybody gets another chance and The Mother is everywhere. While I was definitely feeling grounded, this experience had not come about through a standing posture. I looked around and saw that most of the women were either lying face down around the sea cave, squatting quietly or sitting on the ground with legs apart. I had not observed women doing this during other retreats when both sexes were present. I felt that I was observing something very important about how women make contact and ways that they instinctively ground.

A woman lying next to me had been born with a spinal deformity, which had plagued her with lifelong feelings of isolation and separateness. Stretched out on the ground, she experienced a profound connection with rocks and sea through a sense of the minerals in her bones, knowing that these minerals and trace elements also existed in both rock and seawater. Lying there was an important step for her in healing a series of broken connections.

In later conversations we talked about physicality and the way that women know by a kind of saturating contact. At the beginning of life we know mother, and later father, absorbing their energy through contact. This is a kind of direct knowing. There was something about the way that the women were aligning their bodies in contact with Earth that was different in an all-female setting. The reason, I believe, lies in part in gender differences in the structure of the urogenital diaphragm of the pelvic floor.

These anatomical differences, to some degree, account for a difference in the way that men and women ground. Our frequent squatting postures amongst the women, it appeared, came not only from an absence of chairs, but also from a desire to stretch and relax our inner thigh muscles. I began to speculate that when men are not around there is an absence of sexual tension. Our unconscious response to this is a relaxation of the genitals, which is expressed in a "letting down" or relaxation of the pelvic floor.

I understood that I was observing women actually letting down the pelvic floor onto the ground, often with legs apart. I continued to notice this phenomenon throughout our retreat, women sitting on the ground, on rocks and straddling rocks and ledges. At times, I saw them rock forward in a sitting position to bring alignment upward through their spines and arch their backs to allow more of the perineum into contact with the ground.

Consciously, or unconsciously, they seemed to be experimenting with a sense of absorption and pleasurable connection with Earth. This kind of pelvic grounding has something important to do with letting go. Men urinate standing up, and in order to do this they have to relax the pelvic floor and they do this from a standing position. There is also something very directional about this.

Most Northern American and European women prefer to urinate sitting down. In wilderness situations this can present a problem for women who have difficulty letting the pelvic floor relax to urinate without the familiar contact of a toilet seat or some other form of direct contact with the ground. For females, this is not a particularly directional process. This, for women, is more about letting go.

As we developed our understanding of these gender dynamics, it became clear that there were some trust issues involved. As one woman with a history of sexual violation expressed: "It's important that the earth is stable and that the contact is your choice. You're in control of that contact. And you can titrate and choose. Also the ground is in some ways receptive, no matter how hard the surface is. Actually, I think that the receptivity of earth in allowing the energy down, the stability down, is probably quite important in that process of trust on a physical level, which then gives that information all through the system that trust is possible. The ground allows direct contact ... it can hold you up ... you can relax down into it and it doesn't move out from under you, or up into you. Sitting like that you can take as much time as you can want ... take your own time."

People who have been sexually traumatized often "lose ground." In working with women, both as a body-worker and later as a psychotherapist, I have noticed that in the aftermath of sexual trauma, awareness is often withdrawn from the lower half of their bodies and from the pelvic area in particular. In teaching others about this response, I would say that sexually and pelvically traumatized people "lose their legs." Most of their bodily awareness is thereafter centered above the diaphragm. The energetic task of this dome-shaped muscle then becomes to "keep a lid" on the unwanted feelings and sensations arising from the lower body. As a result many sexually traumatized people suffer a panoply of symptoms involving organs around and below the diaphragm including the stomach, spleen, pancreas, liver and gall bladder.

This concentration of energy above the diaphragm can also lead to headaches, dizziness and other symptoms relating to this imbalance. Lack of awareness in the legs and lower legs in particular, is often a remnant of a thwarted fight-or-flight response, where the person could do neither and froze. This lack of awareness in the legs also impairs defensive responses and paves a way for further trauma. I began to realize the importance of restoring awareness to the lower half of the body, in a gentle way that felt empowering. It wasn't however, until later in the year, after the women's retreat, that I fully understood the role of the pelvic floor in healing sexually traumatized women.

Observing women in the natural world, I began to speculate that some kinds of healing are best done in same-sex settings. During that afternoon at the sea cave, I began to feel that women know a lot about healing other women and that it would be useful to explore more of what we know about that. The women experienced this in numerous ways, which reflected their experiences of exploring both boundaries and merging. As one woman offered: "The rocks were like incredible mirrors especially of the need to slow down, tune in, and become receptive ... not only receptive to them, but to ourselves, to know and be able to feel and sense when we are not receptive and to be able to change that."

"Then, I saw this woman with her body wrapped around a stone and holding on to it. I saw that as immediately healing. Breathing against the stone she could feel her own breath and her own belly. Because the stone doesn't move ... she got to feel herself. Stones help us to feel ourselves. I think some traumatized people don't really know that they are alive, and that is one way to shockingly recognize their own physicality and pulse. And, they also discover breath and their own energy, and it just goes on and on because then they can discover their own spirituality, or maybe not, At least, however, they will have discovered their physicality, their Being. They discover their perimeter and they discover their boundaries. So that, I think, is pretty profound."

The women continued to explore and interact with each other and the cave, someone discovered that an archway that bridged an area between the sea and the top of the cave opening also held another opening. We saw a kind of rock saddle formation with an aperture below that looked directly down into the cavernous depths. The angle of the late afternoon sun cast this area entirely in shadow. "The Dark Cervix," someone offered. "It's a birth rock."

A wealth of intrapsychic material was generated around this experience. Women took turns sitting in a rock cliff saddle, high above the ocean, looking down through a dark cavernous dark orifice to the waters below. For some, it was evocative of feelings around being born. For others, experiences of giving birth, of failed pregnancies, and for a few, feelings about never having had either experience, arrived in wanted or unwanted waves of recognition.

We regrouped for an early sunset walk back to toward camp, carefully stepping among piles of driftwood and flotsam brought forth by the seasonal rhythms of lunar tides. Dinner was ready. After a leisurely meal, we began to drift toward the direction of our yurt. Lit by candlelight from within, our gathering space softly beckoned our participants, like some large paper lantern glowing out in a dark meadow. As agreed, we passed our talking stick and women either talked or they didn't. All of us, we readily acknowledged, for the most part, were still very, very, tired.

LILITH AND EVE

> *"We may listen to each other's stories once again. Most of the stories we are told are written by novelists and screenwriters, acted out by actors and actresses, stories that have beginnings and endings ... remember that the real world is made ofjust such stories. They are a front row seat to the real experience .... Real stories take time. We stopped telling stories when we started to lose that sort of time, pausing time, reflecting time, wondering time ... In telling them, we are telling each other, the human story."*
> Naomi Remen, M. D., *Kitchen Table Wisdom*

First light brought the incessant caws of a pair of ravens. "Ravens!" I called across to Maria's tent. "Good medicine!" she replied. We soon learned that everyone had heard them. Later around our morning fire we read about Raven from her Medicine Card book:
... Ravens announce a change in consciousness. This may involve walking inside the Great Mystery on another path at the edge of time ... Can you accept it as a gift of the Great Spirit ... or will you limit the power of the mystery by explaining it away (Sams a. Carson 1988).

Smart Ravens, I thought. This morning's exercise had to do with our perception of time. The afternoon we would spend exploring the Moon Rock area, which is as evocative and primevally mysterious a place as I have ever been. Our camp was cold and damp beneath a bleak, impenetrable sky. Morning fog clung to us and no one hurried to leave our fire. Summer is foggy season in this part of California. These summer fogs are defined as "advection fogs" because they are generated by a horizontal movement of air. Such conditions exist only in regions where the sea surface is much colder than the air traveling over it. The north central California coast is one of the regions of maximum annual fog frequency in the Northern Hemisphere.

"Where is the sun?" someone asked Maria. "Hiding still," she replied. Maria went to find a long stick and then returned to begin drawing a large circle in some soft dirt near the fire. "Remember when you were a child and you really did believe that you could make the sun come out? Be like a child now, and believe with me, that this big happy picture of our sun will bring the sunshine out." It's only a game. A child's game. Have you forgotten how to play?" to remember a time when I really did believe that the sun te out ifl wanted it to. Maria was having so much fun drawing her happy sun; I let myself pretend that I believed that her game would bring out the sun. And then, naturally, the sun came out. Thinking of Raven, I resisted any temptation to explain this away.

The wind-blown morning air gently dispersed any lingering wisps of fog. I asked each of the women to take some time exploring an area around our campsite and to find a stick of some sort whose length, shape and texture appealed to them. We were to spend our morning working with a variation of Jean Houston's "Yardstick of Time" exercise. As the work of Dr. Humphrey Osmond, Bernard Anson and others have shown, when you change time, you change reality. (Houston 1982).

After the women had found their sticks, I suggested that we gather in the west meadow overlooking the sea. As the women circled in this meadow, I asked them to take some time to settle in and bring their awareness into their bodies, at this place, at this time, in this present moment of *now.* If someone was not able to do this, I asked that they just notice that. I then encouraged them to imagine that their sticks were "time sticks". They were to divide these time sticks into three segments indicating past, present and future. These areas indicating these time zones were entirely arbitrary and their zones not necessarily of equal length. I asked each person to try to determine where on their stick she felt they spent most of her time. Was it here and now, or mostly in the past, or perhaps the future?

I then asked each one to choose one time zone and spend their next thirty minutes somewhere in the surrounding landscape, as if they were actually in the consciousness of that zone. Many people are not aware that they have any options in their perception of time or reality. This exercise is a gentle intervention designed to expand awareness and introduces a sense of options into areas that were previously considered "fixed".

Yael Danieli, as a result of her work with people who have suffered overwhelming life events, postulates a need for linear integration along the *time dimension.* This can be conceptualized as a need for trauma survivors to orient themselves in relationship to past, present and future. This allows for a full perspective of the traumatic experience and their impact on one's life space at any point in time (Danieli 1985).

Reconstructing the inner world of a shattered life requires not only time, but also an ability to remain in a present-oriented state of consciousness long enough to attend to past events. One needs to be present with one's past, long enough, to allow integration of traumatic responses that have remained frozen in time. Here we may find frozen responses that have been long operating outside of conscious awareness.

Response to overwhelming life events can often impair one's ability to respond effectively in present time. Overwhelm and traumatization can cause rupture and possible regression to less overwhelming states of consciousness and a condition of being "stuck" in the past. This essentially adaptive mechanism of the psyche Danieli calls "fixity", which obstructs the normal flow of life. Thus, traumatized people often suffer from distortions in their perceptions of space and time. For many overwhelmed people, the future exists only as a potential for repeating a painful past. Unable to remain in present time, with no future distinct from the past, emotionally wounded people are often caught up in cycles of anxiety and despair.

Wilderness settings, and time spent in the natural world, can serve as an important catalyst and therapeutic setting for reorienting traumatized people. By providing an opportunity to respond in what, for modem people, is a relatively novel and ever changing environment; nature invites the traumatized out of their particular chronic psycho- physiological identification with frozen, numb and trace-like states. This enables them to begin the process of shifting from past-oriented behavior with less fear of an unknown future.

In describing the fragmentation and sense of isolation experienced by emotionally wounded and overwhelmed individuals, psychiatrist R. J. Lifton sees them as suffering a vast breakdown of faith in a larger matrix supportive of life (Lifton 1979). More and more, I carne to understand the degree to which natural settings present an opportunity for temporary re-immersion into a holistic and integrated state of consciousness. In nature, one can reclaim, and renew, half-forgotten physical and emotional knowledge. One is placed in a matrix along with an opportunity to experience, among other things, the spontaneity of weather, cycles of daylight and nightfall, while immersed in surroundings of enormously complex patterns of vegetation, water flow and animal life.

Slowly, our women reassembled and shared some of their perceptions. I then asked them to choose another time zone and to spend another half-hour, or so, out and around in the landscape exploring their experience of that consciousness. They were gone for about a quarter of an hour and then were drawn back to the meadow by a circling of a large number of turkey vultures. Someone counted 24 of them in the sun-filled air above. The women stretched out on the grass and looked up toward a sky, now rich in raptors. Red-tailed hawks soared overhead, casting moving shadows across the tall grasses.

"I love watching the red tails," one woman offered, while leaning toward the group, as if to share a secret. In a voice no louder than a whisper, "I like to imagine that they fly back and forth mending the tears in the upper dimensions of the sky." "Oh, that's a wonderful thought," another said, together with a crushing realization, "but if my husband were here he wouldn't allow you to have it. He would insist that you understand basic aerodynamic principles involving flight patterns of hawks and that it is not possible that they are mending anything."

Is this an instance of "logical battering" or gender miscommunication? A complex question, but for this moment, we settled for simply being grateful that her husband was not there. For now, at least, we were free to offer a poetic or fanciful perception without fear of "correction." It was hot and sunny, and we were all ready for lunch. We returned our time sticks to the campground and prepared to leave for The Moon.

On the Dark Side ofthe Moon

There are several ways to reach the Moon Rock area. This time we chose a steep cliff-side path arising just to the left of Stump Beach. We stepped across a small fresh water stream and began a careful ascent up along a cluster of sandy rock-strewn cliffs. From up along a cliff top we enjoyed a sweeping view of northern California coastline. Chilly indigo and bottle green tides restlessly churned around rocky, surf- battered ledges below. The sea, I am reminded, is always in motion, stirred by Earth's rotations, swept by ever-present winds and subject to gravitational forces of sun and moon.

These cold, element-rich waters harbor abundant plant and animal life. Deep purple and green shades of slippery seaweed and sea wrack, bob and weave across a gently foaming surface. Long slender tangled skeins of amber marine vegetation swirl downward into the murky depths below. Early morning breezes blow fresh with a sting of iodine as we follow a narrow path leading us toward a surreal stretch of barren landscape known as The Moon.

The dry pounded surface of our cliff-side path soon revealed a huge compound of surrealistic rock formations looming, just ahead. One could almost imagine the deep-seated geological forces shift- ing deep within the earth triggering millions of years of creative and destructive upheaval. Oceanic and continental crustal plates collided and then pulled apart with titanic force in order to create this prime- val landscape. No one knows for certain when those plates will shift again. Trusting that for today, at least, there would be no subterranean upheavals, our explorations continued. Salt-rimmed tide pools were all around, along with hollows, cavities and a sensuous variety of mysterious crevices. We allowed ourselves to just wander amongst an abundance of polished rocks suggestive of nipples, breasts and other human and animal bodily forms.

This moonscape was richly endowed with large, rather fantastic formations such as those, which we named "the dinosaur's rib cage" and the "belly of the whale". An ominous cluster of jagged rocks towering high above treacherous waves became the shattered wings of "a fallen angel". These large, primordial formations were surrounded by and interspersed with hauntingly delicate, almost skeletal traceries of honeycomb lacework and hieroglyphic patterns etched into a number of sandstone outcroppings.

Our "dinosaur's rib cage" drew quite a bit of attention. Dinosaurs were primitive, cold-blooded creatures whose instinct-driven brains mandated a totally survival-based existence. They perished as a result of forces beyond their control. Humans may very well share a similar fate, or paradoxically, we may perish, as a result of forces within our control. It may be that this threat of extinction has something to do with our culture's current fascination with dinosaurs. This fascination is apparent, not only in the popularity of *Jurassic Park* but in Maya Angelou's poem at the inauguration of President William Jefferson Clinton in January of 1993:

A Rock, a River, a Tree

Hosts to species long
departed Marked the
mastodon,
The dinosaur, which left dried tokens
of their sojourn

here

On our planet
floor,
Any broad alarm of their hastening
doom Is lost in the gloom of dust and
ages.
But, today, the Rock cries out to us,
clearly, Forcefully,
Come you may stand upon my
Back and face your distant destiny ...
The Rock cries out to us
today, You may stand
upon me;
But do not hide your face.

Angelou 1993

For those of us who work with people who have encountered the violent side of human nature, its seems important not only to accept the reality of evil, but also to develop a perspective on those forces of change which are larger than good and evil, or us and "them". While we humans do seem to have some control over our lives, we also seem to be powerless victims of another order.

In *Re-imagination of the World* (1991) William Irwin Thompson asks us to imagine a Sierra Club meeting of dinosaurs watching a comet coming in to cause what is now known as the Cretaceous Extinction. Naturally, they are worried, and so they hold an emergency meeting of dinosaurs to deal with their situation. Now, what they would try to figure out is how to make their world safe for dinosaurs. These anxious sauropods would definitely not be able to imagine a world in which the space that they vacate becomes filled with warm blooded mammals (Thompson a.

Spangler 1991).

The Cretaceous extinction represents a clear instance of a time when forces of destruction erupted with all of their ugliness and horror during which 70 % of planetary life was annihilated. Nevertheless, like seeds popping up after a forest fire or soil growing rich after a volcanic eruption, life rebounded and mammals did evolve into spaces left by dinosaurs. While all of this took place on a scale vastly beyond an individual ego, one can still find some reassurance in the notion that forces of life seem to be more than equal to forces of destruction (Thompson a. Spangler 1991).

It seems however, that this premise might be severely tested during this current time period which scientists have termed "The Sixth Extinction". Fifty percent of our world's flora and fauna could disappear before the end of this century. Previous extinctions have occurred five times since complex life emerged, and each time caused by a natural disaster. This Sixth Extinction is happening because of the collective actions of *Homo sapiens* (Leaky a. Lewin 1995).

The dinosaur formation was large enough for the women to actually stand on its "back" and ease into some whole body version of contact with a primordial shape. Here and there conversations were again leading back to the subject of origins, evolution and strategies for survival. Time passed in silence as Maria stretched herself out on her back, directly under the protection of a smooth round overhang. Eventually she spoke:

"Rocks are very ancient beings. They have been on the Earth for so long that they have much to teach us. So, what I am doing is just lying here, slowing down and becoming receptive ... just being with them. Rock messages don't come in thought form. They come into my body as softening up. Opening up. Not having to push so myself so hard. Because they are rocks and they have been there for so long they don't have to do much. They don't move much. They are prints, encoded records of what's been going on here on Earth for eons. They have felt it all and everything is recorded within them."

Maria remained there resting and being receptive while the other women roamed the area, now and then pausing to feel various surface textures, shapes and temperature variations. They found an abundance of inside shapes and outside shapes. Some explored feelings of being inside various kinds of enclosures that they had explored from the out- side. One participant became intrigued with her idea of curling up and experiencing connection, to be small and round inside of something:

"Even if it's touching my whole back, just to be inside that enclosure reminds me of the womb. I think that one of the things that's fun about that is that you can have different sizes ... like different sizes of development that you could be during fetal development. I like the prospect of filling out an enclosure that was relatively small and feel actual contact, physical contact of that around your back, arms and legs. And then, you could be in a big enclosure, lil<e the dinosaur's rib cage and think about being a tiny zygote in a beginning in which you would have plenty of room to move and stretch and explore.

And, then, you could be also be on top of and underneath the rocks, as well as tall as and taller than those rocks and have it all be safe."

Rather unexpectedly, we found ourselves facing a stone formation that soon revealed an interesting cave, located within a large fissure of shadowy monolithic rock face looming near the water's edge. This territory was definitely "the dark side of the moon." Almost immediately, this intriguing aperture became "Lilith's Cave".

For several millennia Eve dominated Western culture and Lilith has scarcely been permitted to exist. In recent decades, the feminist movement has brought Lilith into a light where her suffering outrage can be acknowledged and her positive qualities have an opportunity to overcome the negativity that comes from exclusion and repression. Turning to mythological sources may provide some insight and understanding of those core beliefs, which have fostered dissonance, lack of understanding, and no small degree of violence between men and women (Christ a. Plaskow 1992, Plaskow a. Christ 1989; see also Downing 1981, 1990).

With the emergence of a wild woman archetype, popularized by Clarissa Pinkola Estes in *Women Who Run With the Wolves,* it is not surprising that the story of Lilith, the defiantly autonomous first wife of Adam, should become popular in contemporary feminist literature. According to Hebrew legend, Lilith fled from Eden in order to avoid having to submit to domination by Adam. Ever since her flight, she has been given to dwelling in wild and uninhabited places. Her favorite resting-place was imagined to be a cave by the sea (Schwartz 1988).

The legend of Lilith can be traced through Jewish literary tradition from its biblical inception and recounting in The Talmud on through versions found in The Midrash (Jewish folk stories) and then retold as medieval folklore and echoed in some Hassidic tales. This multifaceted legend came into being as a commentary on one passage in the Bible, "male and female, He created them" (Genesis 1: 27). This passage was interpreted by the rabbis to mean that creation of man and woman was simultaneous, whereas later accounts of the creation of Adam and Eve appear to be sequential (Ausubel 1948).

Working on their assumption that every word in the

Bible was literally true, rabbis interpreted this contradiction to mean that this first passage referred to the creation of Adam's first wife, whom they named "Lilith" *(Lilah* is the Hebrew word for night and Lilith's hair was said to be as black as darkness). The other passage, they believed, referred to the creation of Eve. This initiated the long legend of Lilith whose name actually appears in the Bible only once in a passage from Isaiah, "Yea, Lilith shall repose here (Isaiah 34: 14) referring probably to a Babylonian demon of the night.

Within post-biblical texts, a few references to Lilith are found in The Talmud, where she is described as a darkly tressed demoness (Schwartz 1988, Charlesworth 1983). A demoness with identical characteristics is found in an apocryphal text, *The Testament of Solomon.* The earliest version, however, is a legend that portrays all essential aspects of Lilith in the seventh century *Alphabet of Ben Sira* of Persian or Arabic origin. This version tells how Yahweh created Adam and Lilith out of the same clay and Lilith became Adam's wife long before Eve was created out of his rib. This Lilith was beautiful and seductive with long flowing hair and wings of an angel. Nevertheless, Adam and Lilith bickered endlessly over matters large and small. It would appear that Lilith was the original feminist who refused to allow Adam to dominate her in any way. After watching animals copulate, Adam is believed to have demanded that Lilith lie beneath him and submit. When he attempted to force her, the story goes, she flew away to a cave by the sea (Plaskow a. Christ 1989, Paiva 1989).

As the tragedy continues, Adam then appealed to God who then sent three angels, Senoy, Sansenoy and Semangeloff, to find Lilith and return her to Adam. These dutiful angels threatened to drown her in the Red Sea, but Lilith would not yield and they had to let her go. This wild first wife of Adam then announced that she would avenge all wrongs done to her by snatching the souls of helpless infants. So widely known is this legend that amulets bearing the names of the three an- gels were used to protect newborn children and are even evoked today in some Orthodox Jewish circles. There is also a tradition wherein a ring was drawn in charcoal in birthing rooms and written inside were the words "Adam and Eve: Out, Lilith!" (Schwartz 1988).

The English word lullaby is probably derived from the Hebrew *Liliaabi* (Lilith be gone). Legend has it that ever since her flight from Eden, Lilith has been given a dwelling in wild and uninhabited places. She has flown as head of hosts of evil spirits, a storm goddess and nocturnal demon, howling her hatred through the voice of a screech owl. Lilith dances in the ruins of empty cities. For nomadic Hebrews, Lilith was a voice howling over mounds of dead and vanished civilizations, a female voice living in the desolation of male vanities (Thompson 1978).

Once a character was brought into being, the rabbis sought to discern, or if necessary, invent, his or her history. So it is with Lilith who, from a rabbinical perspective, represents the negative side of woman. Lilith is assertive, seductive, wild and ultimately destructive. Eve was portrayed as a devoted wife and mother. Eve is passive, faithful and supportive, a positive polarity in contrast to negative aspects of Lilith. The :first wife is held as a devastating incarnation of lust, despite the story that she refused sexual coercion, who leads unsuspecting men into sin. Accusations of a lustful nature, also consigns her character to that of a child-destroying witch devoid of any maternal feeling. This interpretation, as far as I can discern, makes no attempt to explain, how, within this framework of understanding; they explain "The Fall". In this version, wherein Eve, under the influence of a serpent, is bla- med for seducing Adam to bite into an apple, which represented the "Forbidden Fruit of Knowledge."

If Lilith served no other purpose than to resolve a contradiction in the biblical text, such an extensive legend with so many ramifications would never have come into being. From a Jungian perspective, Lilith serves as a projection of the negativities and desires of the rabbis who created her. It is clear that Lilith stories held great power for those who told them. Much of this power came from the fact that these supernatural tales embody universal fears and fantasies (Dallett 1991).

The story of Lilith also reveals a great deal about the workings of the folk process. This very old legend splits off into several sub-legends which give birth to multiple variants which are embellished and retold until they bear little resemblance to the original. Nevertheless, various versions of Lilith find resonance with Western women who continue to face a reality in which a negative, primal aspect of woman, not interested in childbearing, has been split off by a patriarchal consciousness where she has remained in exile (Thompson 1978). Lilith's demand for autonomy cost her dearly. This aspect of the feminine has been seen only as demonic and without regard to the suffering of one whose mate, "created of the same substance", home, and Garden of Eden, passed to another. A rare exception to the demonic view of Lilith appears in a lengthy 19th century poem, *Lilith, The Legend of the First Woman* by Ada Langsworthy Collier (l885). Here is a brief excerpt:

"These many days I weary of the sighs,
"Know Lilith that I alone rule Paradise"
... Wrought herfull heart to tears.
"Sweet peace," she said
"Alas lies slain!"

With musing worn she brake
at last her silence, and to Adam spake:
"... I fly,
to seek my home in other lands. For why
should Lilith wait since Adam's empty state?"
More dear he holds than Lilith desolate?

"... I may not hinder thee," the angel
sighed,
"No soul unwilling may here abide."
Slow swung the verdant gate neath saddest eyes
... Lilith forever lost fair Paradise.

While Collier's remarkable poem holds compassion for the tragedy of Lilith's exile, not until recent decades has a desire for, and recognition of any need for, reconciliation surfaced into cultural consciousness. In this respect, it may be that the need for reconciliation is not only between Adam and Lilith, but also between Lilith and Eve. The phenomenological studies of Bert Hellinger have demonstrated over and again, in his Systemic Constellation Work, the disruptive influences of those who are excluded and disrespected.

According to Hellinger, marital relationships that ignore or fail to respect a previous partner will experience disruptive influences between husband and wife, which may also impact their children. Hellinger finds much support for this observation, not only in clinical demonstrations, but also draws upon myth and fairy-tales to illustrate this truth. An obvious example is the "child hating witch" that the Thirteenth Fairy became, cursing a newborn child, after she was excluded from a christening celebration of Briar Rose, also known as "Sleeping Beauty".

Some years later I had a series of opportunities to spend time in conversation with Bert Hellinger and explore his thoughts about men, women and war, and the war between men and women. "It's very simple, you see," he explained, "it's all about balance and respect and proper order. There is no need for power struggle. A woman needs to follow her man into his life, his family, his language and his religion. In return, the purpose of the masculine must be to serve the feminine."

Lilith, of course, was never able to yield and remained unaware of the tremendous power of receptivity. Adam did not respect his wife. Eve did not understand the necessity of honoring Lilith as the first partner of her husband and was fated to follow her, along with Adam, into exile from Eden. Like Lilith, Eve was blamed for the tragedy of exile.

It may be that by "dreaming the myth on" we can move toward healing both the exiled aspects of the feminine and some of the alienation and distrust between the sexes. Reconciliation with the negative manifestations of woman might begin with recognition that in Judea-Christian traditions Lilith and Eve continue to represent polar aspects of woman. One could also view Lilith as a shadow and/*or* complement of Eve with both representing primal feminine energy patterns. As long as Lilith lives unconsciously in women under patriarchal repression, she is often demonic. Ignored and disrespected, Lilith's presence can be felt as depression and an abysmal agony of helplessness and futility. Unacceptable desire, potentially transformative destructive energy, and unacceptable autonomy, such as the need for separateness and assertion, may be split off and turned against the self. Another danger is that, with the presence of Lilith, a woman may unconsciously identify with those qualities that culture rejects as ineffective and inferior, forcing her to introvert through a negative sense of uniqueness (Dallett 1991).

In *Saturday's Child,* Jungian analyst, Janet Dallett observes that in actress June Havoc's description of the women in her family, one can sense the presence of Lilith as their ebullient energies were ground down and soured.

"All the women of our family ... had a common strain of ambition and strength and bitter independence. They married early, divorced quickly, and in the end succumbed to alcohol or drugs or madness. They wanted total freedom and since then were hideously frustrated. Men were a convenience to them; they had an inability to enjoy love."

On the other hand, lived consciously, the archetype of Lilith may provide more productive options. Reflecting on the legend of Lilith, Dallett sees her as an independent woman who only wanted equal status with her husband. Lilith didn't turn mean until the male power interests ganged up on her. Dallett does not blame Lilith for refusing to give in to them. If her husband, a patriarchal God and three angels kept trying to tell her how wrong she was, she would, she said, have done the same (ibid.). Yet, one is left to wonder if there might have been a somewhat more creative outcome to this ultimately destructive power struggle. The more Dallett thought about it, the clearer it became to her, that the archetype of Lilith must be buried in every psyche in the Judeo-Christian world, men and women alike, filling us with horror and shame at the rage and vengefulness we harbor in our depths.

Because her independent spirit was rejected at the very beginning of the Judeo-Christian tradition, it became perverse. The repressed Lilith in each of us takes revenge by "killing children", that is, by attacking whatever is young and undeveloped in ourselves and others. Having been abused, she becomes abusive, embodying that mean streak that will kick a cat, or yell at a child, because young children and small animals cannot fight back. With cutting and sarcastic remarks, she can annihilate fragile new life before it can grow strong enough to survive her contempt. She is manipulative and misuses sex for power. "If you cannot express love", cautions Dallett, "because you feel too vulnerable, if you are afraid to care lest you become dependent, look for Lilith" (ibid.)

In the *Zohar,* a central work of Hebrew mysticism, a theory develops that Adam was originally composed of both male and female elements. This composite hermaphroditic being originally existed with two body fronts with Adam in front and a female counterpart attached at the back. They were eventually separated. In this version Lilith appears literally behind Adam, then metaphorically re-emerges as his shadow (Berg 2002).

This Lilith also lives in the psyches of men as well as women. She may lead a man beyond the traditional Adam-and-Eve kind of marriage into a relationship where dominance is not the issue. A man whose feminine aspect has a strong Lilith component will tend to find attraction in the Lilith within a woman. These Lilith qualities will not make him comfortable, as an Eve type would. However, Lilith has the power to transform, for she serves the development of a man's individuality, not conventionally stereotyped male attitudes (Dallett 1991).

This potentially healing and transformational aspect of Lilith was present in many of the so-called "Bush Vets", or returning Vietnam veterans who, in feeling excluded and disrespected, found solace in the wilderness settings rather than in urban civilization. One of these veterans, whom I met during my time with Mountain Air, expressed these thoughts in a letter addressing the subject of

"Men, Women and War":

"... having been hurt and disempowered by the male power structure (the fathers of our country, etc.) having been witness to the devastation unleashed by the military industrial complex, I found it very difficult to participate in that system ... even for my own survival. A real problem, so I isolated and worked on developing consciousness ... hanging out with demons and animals in the wilderness and turning to instinctive power. Like Lilith, I was howling over the mounds of dead and vanished civilizations. Unlike Lilith, I am a man ... double trouble! Reconciling the opposites within myself was the first order of business ...

As a man, trying to give recognition to the Lilith energy by aligning ... with women possessed of Lilith energy, I would run the risk of asking them to carry it ... but, if they carry it for me, I keep them from achieving balance. I become the controlling male, unbalanced ... and my unconscious Lilith goes to war. If I embody Lilith, I am at odds with 'the monuments of business, civilization and technology' even as they appear in the masculine aspect of women ... and so, I again become the oppressor and controller, denying recognition and achievement. So, again, balancing internally is crucial, otherwise it gets acted out, and men and women war against each other."

W. I. Thompson attaches a broader significance to the reconciliation with Lilith which he believes is now going on in the male psyche. In his view, Lilith has returned out of the collective unconsciousness at the end of a civilizational cycle and at the end of a period of masculine domination. The first response of Man is to be terrified of her, for he sees Her as She, the Raw Savage, Bitch Goddess, Destroyer of Men and embodiment of entropy. In the ancient Babylonian creation myth of *Enuma Elish* the great male god Marduk, tore the Great Mother Goddess Tiamat, apart, in order to build his masculine citadel of Babylon. Now, however, Thompson believes, as the goddess draws back the dismembered pieces of her body to regain her ancient life, she is pulling Babylon to pieces. And then, therefore, men fearing the chaos of the feminine expressed in the form of wild and uncontrollable nature, seek to assert order and control (Thompson 1978).

Thompson speculates that with the return of Lilith, men fear the end of civilization and the death of all of their great cities and industries. These terrors of masculine imagination are very much projections which overlook beneficent aspect of the Dark Feminine. Lilith also represents an opportunity for release from old modes of patriarchal relationship to technological civilization. If we persist in holding tightly on to order, control and repression, then her return IS terrifying.

The reconciliation with Lilith is not only an issue between men and women. Lilith represents a need for reconciliation between the opposites of order and chaos, technology and instinct, civilization and savagery, culture and nature. In male industrial civilizations there were iron walls or compartments which separated nature from culture, death from life, irrational from rational, male from female. Perhaps what is needed is something like osmotic membranes, rather than solid barriers through which information from polarities can be exchanged, with due respect for a need for some boundaries.

If we are lucky, the meeting of these opposites can be more of a marriage than a war. The interface between opposites, male and female, conscious and unconscious, civilization and nature, can become vehicles of transformation. Thompson also reminds us that with the many and maddening variations of a single myth, one is forced to consider the fact that mythology is interested in paradoxes, opposites and transformations, the deep structure of consciousness, and not a surface structure of facts and sensory perceptions. Variations and threads of a single myth running through a myriad of twistings and turnings serves to prevent us from settling down with easy answers (ibid.).

In many parts of our world, however, women have been faced with a belief system in which qualities valued in women have often been defined in relation the masculine: the good nurturing wife, docile agreeable daughter and gently supportive or bright achieving partner. Over time, Janet Dallett's Jungian wisdom has served as a valued literary guide through the feminine realms of an archetypal underworld. In *When the Spirits Come Back* (r988) she laments the pain involved in accepting this collective model:

"We mutilate, depotentiate, silence and enrage ourselves trying to compress our souls into it, just as many of our grandmothers deformed their fully breathing bodies with whalebone corsets for the sake of an ideal" (Dallett 1988).

In Western tradition, women were faced with a reality in which the negative, instinctive, primal aspect of the "Dark Feminine" represented by Lilith has been split off by patriarchal consciousness, where she has remained in exile. Lived consciously, one might imagine a some- what different experience for those possessed of qualities attributed to Lilith. Her demand for equality and autonomy has been considered negative and destructive. Only recently has there been a compassion for the tragedy of Lilith's exile. Not until recent decades has a desire for, and recognition of a need for, reconciliation surfaced into cultural consciousness. It may be by doing what Jung calls "dreaming the myth on" that we can move toward healing both the exiled aspects of the wounded feminine and some of the alienation and distrust between the sexes. Those of us who work with abused, estranged and abusive women, certainly do feel the presence of Lilith. The language of archetype and myth that describes her so vividly also holds important insights into that which is needed to directly address the nature of her suffering (Dallett 1991).

Several women were gathered in the area above "Lilith's cave." One, I noticed, was wearing a sweater vest woven in a dark pattern of whales. She was also wearing whale earrings and a whale pendant. Whales. "Do you ever feel," I asked, "like you want to wail?" "Oh, yes," she replied, amused and amazed at the clarity with which she was wearing her metaphor, "but I never have, and I don't know how."

Maria asked her if she wanted "to go wailing". She did and so did several others. We went down a sloping rock ledge to the entrance to Lilith's Cave. Some of us chose to remain outside the cave and the rest went on in. It was damp and cold inside a rough rock chamber, tomblike and definitely evocative of the underworld. I thought of Susan Griffin writing about the nature of caves in *Women and Nature: The Roaring Inside of Her* (1978):

"Where we meet our outcast selves ... Where we go into darkness. Where we embrace darkness. Where we lie close to darkness, breathe when darkness breathes and find darkness inside ourselves ...The shape of a cave, we say or the shape of a labyrinth. The way that we came here was dark. Space seemed to close in on us ... Our voices echoed off the walls ..." (Griffin 1978).

Seated on this sloping rock ledge, Maria began slowly, rhythmically rocking. The women did likewise and a low moaning sound emerged from the group. Waves crashed onto rocks around us and the moaning surged out into long wailing laments of siren-like intensity. Waves of sound rose and fell in undulant rhythms as the women found a commonality and comfort in their expression. The sound of our voices reverberated up, around and out through the rock walls. Women exploring other parts of the moonscape paused to listen and resonate with this ancient song of the wounded feminine. As the intensity of sound increased, a group of small dark crabs scuttled out from under nearby rocky ledges and crevices. Tilting slightly on delicately armored legs, they extended their eyestalks in rapt attention, like some timeless presence of empathic mourners. When the sound subsided, they slid back into hiding. This unexpected participation of another life form in this event was especially poignant for all of us.

As homeopath Kat Shea expressed: "It was a most amazing thing to have a crab/hurnan interaction through sound. Not a directed sound intended to train, like a whistle, coo, or Ah, but a sound they resonated with ... and then a bunch of them carne out, about 8 or ro! As soon as the wailing was over, they disappeared. Remarkable!"

As in the previous experience with the sea cavern, resonating with sound was especially important. This woman's words echoed many of the others.

"Sitting outside the cave when the women were wailing, I saw the sounds go up into a whirlwind, catching the breezes and circling the Earth, joining in communion with all women in some healing way, bringing back around their wailing, empowerment, rising up, out of hiding and repression.

I am always drawn to caves, it's like the womb or something ... when we were there in Lilith's Cave, right at the water edge, I crawled up into the middle of the cave.

When the women started wailing, I decided that rather than try to make the sounds myself that I really just needed to *take in* what was happening all around me. I was just quiet and I felt the sounds swirling all around the walls of the cave, absorbing them and then wrapping them in sound. It was really, really, a healing and nurturing experience. I had the energy of the cave and the energy of the women, all together. It was a *whole* experience".

While I needed to be in an enclosed area to do that, there was also this opening out to the sea. And the "mourning crabs" coming out to join us was especially healing.

The "waters of life" were getting higher with each wave, and we left for higher ground. The wailing expedition was a success. "I never thought that wailing could be empowering," someone said, as we headed back toward camp. Circled in our yurt that night, women spoke of "women things", life and loss and relationships, vanity, aging, and, of course, men.

That night I dreamed again of edges, waves upon water, atmosphere swirling above the vastness of the depths below and coming together along some unending shore. Turbulent spirals of evolutionary process danced their way, as though driven, into patterns entirely new, and, as yet, unknown.

I hear the voice of T. S. Eliot:

Other echoes
Inhabit the
garden. Shall we
follow?

Descansos

Descansos, mark death sites and dark times, but they are also love notes to the suffering and this can be transformative.
Clarissa Pinkola Estes, *Women Who Run With Wolves*

While gathered around our morning fire, I read aloud a passage from *Women Who Run With Wolves* (Estes 1992):

"There is a time in life, usually in mid-life, when a woman has to make a decision- possibly the most important decision ofher fUture life- about whether to be bitter or not. Women often come to this ... at a point where they are full up to their ears with everything and they've "had it" and the last straw has broken the camel's back and they are pissed off and pooped out."

This passage struck a chord and we agreed to spend at least part of our day, with some journaling work. Estes believes that a psyche that has lived a long time accumulates debris and there is need for cleansing and renewal. *Descansos,* she explains are symbols that mark a death. This concept of *Descansos* evolved from the handmade little white crosses by the roadways of Old Mexico, New Mexico, southern Colorado and Arizona. They can also be found on the edges of cliffs along many scenic, but treacherous roadways in Greece, Italy and other Mediterranean areas. These symbols of death mark, right there, in that place, someone's life journey came to an unexpected end. Perhaps it was an automobile accident, or heat exhaustion or a fight. Something happened at that place that altered that person's life and other people's lives forever. Women, Estes says, die thousands of deaths before middle age.

We have gone in this direction or that and have been cut off. We have hopes and dreams that have also been cut of£ While all of these things deepen individuation, encourage growing up, growing out, and becoming awake, aware and conscious, they are also profound tragedies that have to be grieved as such.

To make *Descansos* means taking a look at your life and marking where the small deaths, and the big deaths, have taken place. Participants are invited to make a time line from infancy to the present, where pieces and parts of the self and one's life have died along the way. Roads not taken, paths that were cut off, ambushes, and betrayals could be marked with crosses or other symbols to mark those places that should have been mourned and still need to be mourned (ibid.).

The women were invited to choose an event from their time line and create a way of marking and releasing the suffering using the natural world around them. We packed our lunch materials and set off hiking over long meadow paths on our way back toward the Moon Rock area. Doing *Descansos* was an intensely private experience for most of the women that chose to do them. One woman, however, was willing to share her process. She came to our retreat feeling both emotionally and physically weak. She was, as she said, "as close as I could be to dying and still be up and around." Doing *Descansos* went a long way toward healing of broken connections for her.

"I had so many losses, so many deaths of babies. I made a chain of yellow wildflowers and it wasn't a very secure chain, but the connections were there. I have living children and dead children. I wasn't able to make the connection, once my child was born; the one who died at birth. He was just taken away before I had a chance to hold him. That was one of things that I was trying rework, the physical connection with him, and that he fits in my family between the other children. He is in the middle of my children. And, he was not honored. I did not know how to do that. I didn't know how to say goodbye ... I didn't know what it meant that he died. There is something about the dying yellow flowers that pass so quickly, the delicacy and the transient nature. You really have to appreciate them at the moment, especially if you pick them. If you pick them and make a chain of them, they die very quickly. Wildflowers go so quickly. In making the chain, I was able to have the connection of thinking about his spirit with a living part of the Earth, and then leaving it with the Earth, which I didn't get to do when the baby died.

So, I guess, to me the yellow flowers have in some way enriched all of the spirits on the same level: the dead one, who is not on the earth, and the living ones that are. So, there is a connection that does not disappear. Also, another part of this was making the connection that I no longer wanted the connection with my husband. In making this connection, I began the process of letting go and of letting something die, in order to live. It was at that time that I made the choice to live."

For another, sitting out on a cluster of rocks overlooking the ocean, the experience of *Descansos* wasn't consciously planned. As I was walking along the cliffs she waved me over and asked me to sit with her. She later described her experience:

"That day amazes me. What led me up to it was the smell of the sea and how strongly it reminded me of my father, who was a raging alcoholic, and all the fishing trips when he took me along. This smell of fish and of the sea reminded me of always having to 'walk on eggshells' around him and how much I hated that."

As she was talking, I noticed the pale shards of sea bird eggs lying in a rocky crevice almost hidden from view. I reached down into the crevice and offered her a handful of eggshells. "Then you (laughing) make these eggshells appear, so I smashed them and crunched and crushed them and threw them right off the cliff It was great! And, it stays with me. Now I recognize when I am walking on eggshells with someone and I just imagine myself back to that rock and that cliff and I do it again. It has been very healing, a kind of coming into my own ... allowing myself to walk on the ground instead of on eggshells. You know ... feeling my own feet on the ground."

Another woman felt unable to do any *Descansos* at the time of the re- treat. Being there was the beginning of a process of realizing that she felt that she needed to something of that nature.

"When I returned I did a lot of it ... and had celebration around it and gratitude for the experience of being able to do that. Some of it was around babies and babies I didn't have and babies that I did have that have been hurt. Somehow it was about parts of myself that had been snared and quartered and buried ... and burying them rather than carrying them around with me."

Doing *Descansos* takes time and patience and willingness to be gentle with oneself in laying to rest those aspects of oneself that were on their way somewhere and never arrived. *Descansos* mark death sites and dark times, but they are also love notes to the suffering and this can be transformative. There is a lot to be said, Estes says, for pinning things to the earth so that they don't follow us around (ibid.).

Around the Fire: Fatigue and Fear of Accusation

Each evening we would gravitate toward the restless nest of warm fire. From time immemorial women have been keepers of the hearth, tenders of fire and the light and warmth of the feminine consciousness that turned a cave into a home. "The heat of the feminine," writes Mary Hugh Scott in *The Passion of Being Woman* (1991), "... is like the fire woman used to change grain and water into bread, clay into stone, and raw meat into food. The heat of her sexual fire turned a cold bed into a place of comfort."

Circled beneath the vault of night sky, we looked out from our spot, here on this third planet from the sun, and settled in for some conversation and exchange of ideas before retiring. No one seemed inclined to stay up very late. "Why," I asked, "are women so tired?" "A better question," someone offered, "might be, 'Why do we feel that we have to do it all?'" Modem woman in our Western world is a blur of activity, pressured to be all things to all people. We live in a fast paced, demanding world very different from the one we grew up in, now, seemingly light years from our parents and grandparents.

"From my perspective," Maria said, "Euro-American women are out of touch with their natural rhythms and cycles. In many indigenous cultures, and Native American cultures in particular, it is understood that during menses women need to take a break from daily responsibilities. They retire to 'moon lodges' for a time of rest and renewal in the company of other women. This also provides men with valued time to be spent with their own gender. This time that men and women spend apart is believed to improve relations between the sexes." Many resonated with the need for "time out". Women need time out. I thought about tribal women isolating during their periods. Body clock time out. How they need to go and moon watch. They need to be separate with their feelings and with their ragged edges in a way that other women understand and that doesn't need any extraneous stimulation from the culture.

I had a client who said that she needed to have her own clock. She said that she had a clock and her husband had a clock and their clocks didn't match. "If you can," she suggested, "synchronize your rhythm to the rhythm of the day, by using nature to synchronize your internal timing with something larger than yourself. It's like we're the moon in the Earth's gravitational field and there is a spinning realm that's separate from its orbiting rhythm, but it's relational."

While the women agree the "time out" each month for rest and renewal sounds like a wonderful idea, it is just not feasible in modem American culture. Fatigue was a major topic of discussion. Ibis woman expressed a sense of exasperation that was felt by others as well.

"I felt like this is a group of wounded healers ... and that made me angry. I remember thinking, Oh my God, if this is the state of the healers in our society, then we are in really bad shape! But, on the other hand I can say that it is reassuring that there are ways like this that people can resource themselves and that healers can and do get resourced." Several were alarmed that we could allow ourselves to become so tired.

"Well, we certainly talked about fatigue. There was a physical aura of fatigue ... women dying and maybe not dying, but being so exhausted that there is an air of vulnerability that had intensity to it. There are a lot of people there choosing to live or die. It was shocking and fear instilling that all of these people, myself included, would allow this level of depletion."

Some began exploring reasons for fatigue. "I can only speak for myself. I think that I get tired because I am afraid that if I stop doing things for other people first and myself second, that I will not deserve to be alive. I think just being in nature, for me, is one of the ways just to be alive and realize that it is enough."

This need to justify one's existence was an underlying reason that several women were able to articulate. As one lady described: "It is an internalized sense of not deserving to live. Women come into this world, for the most part, having to justify their existence because they are women, because they are not men, because they are not go- ing to become warriors or go out and hunt for food ...What woman does has been considered secondary for so long that everybody has just taken that in."

Another spoke of "compassion fatigue" experienced by many. "My family is so needy and in so much pain and anger that they have to take up so much space and there is no space for me. The neediness of the world is so big ... it is screaming to be tended to and doesn't allow any space. If you have any amount of compassion then it is really hard. It's too much and overwhelming, and if you try to put up boundaries to protect yourself, it takes too much energy to keep from getting sucked dry of everything that you have, and it is all very tiring.

I used to be so compassionate and so able to give but I got to the point where it was just all gone. It hasn't been until I've allowed com- passion for myself, which is one of the things I've learned at the retreat, about women needing nurturing, that I could funnel the compassion back to myself ... and that I don't have to be drained."

Women's need to be nurtured was widely

acknowledged. Women are so good at nurturing, and what they really need is nurturing.

"I was surprised. A workshop where I could just be! So, I slept soundly. I was exhausted from working so much ... family, clients, teaching, traveling. Most of the women who were tired were from big cities, big clienteles. The retreat was a big turnaround for me. I am letting go of things I don't need and so much efforting of everything." And again: "I found that women want to be ... when they have the opportunity ... able to kick back and be nurtured. That's what seemed to happen most of the time. Everybody needs to rest, like sponges, just absorbing the beauty of places."

Another recalled collecting her inner and outer resources with time out in nature, as a child. "I grew up in the country. As a little girl, when I needed to mind myself again, I would pack up my suitcase, put in my grandmother's quilt, a peanut butter and jelly sandwich and a book, maybe water, and walk as far away as it felt safe to walk. I usually kept the house in sight, but it still felt far away. And, I go and sit underneath a tree and spread out my blanket, put out my sandwich, bring out my book, and sit and look at the top of the tree from underneath. Walking to the place and then having time to sit was a way that I got myself back and resourced myself to go back to my family situation."

All in all, the value of tuning in to the instinctive feminine and the resources in nature were abundantly clear. However, those who study history know that close associations between women and nature are sometimes suspect and dangerous to manifest. Almost all of the women at our gathering were involved in some sort of alternative healing or therapeutic practice. Our evening conversations would quite naturally include topics of healing practices, herbs and remedies.

On the last night of the retreat, the women instinctively quieted when forest rangers slowly drove past our campsite several times. A chill of fear rippled almost imperceptibly through our circle. Women alone in the forest, without men, closely circled around a fire. Some of us never married, had left their marriages or were contemplating leaving. Age qualified a few of us as wise women, or "crones", and hags, even after a few days without makeup and mirrors.

The rangers' curiosity (or suspicions) momentarily awakened an age-old fear of accusation and the charges of witchcraft. My thoughts turned to those difficult times when any woman living alone, as spinster or widow, with an herb garden and a cat was vulnerable to charges of sorcery. An exploration of this subject of women and nature and women's spirituality should, I believe, consider the reality of the witch hunts. While some 20 percent of those persecuted were male, during the "Burning Times" from 1170 through to the 1700's, witches were mostly women who were believed to have a great spiritual power and an intimate knowledge of plants and their uses for healing (Daly 1978).

Paracelsus, the "father of modem medicine" burned his texts in 1527 and confessed that he had learned all that he knew from a sorceress. Historically, witch hunts, coincided with the professionalization and rise of medicine. In addition, the massacre of hundreds of thou- sands of women served to sever the continuity of women's culture and knowledge of midwifery and natural healing (Galland 1990).

Only recently have we begun to take health and healing back into our own hands. Much of what has been considered "witchcraft" was in fact native healing modalities, which are being revived as part of holistic and alternative medicine. Women are now allowed to train as physicians, and delivery by midwives is becoming increasingly common. During the "Burning Times" if a woman dared to cure without having studied, she was considered to be a witch. And, because women were not permitted to study, any female healer was by definition a witch (Ehremeich a. English 1973).

Women's sexuality also damned them as witches. It is instructive to read a 14th century official church document *The Malleus Maleficarum* (The Hammer of Witches) written by two Dominican priests during an early phase of the witch craze. Reprinted l4 times before 1521 and another 15 times after 1576, this document contributed to an overwhelmingly negative focus on women during the following centuries with inflammatory statements such as "... all witchcraft comes from carnal lust, which in women is insatiable" (Daly 1978).

Witch-burning "caught on" and spread like wildfire. Trevor Roper (1969) describes it as an explosive force. "The witch hysteria grew terribly after the Renaissance, peaked during the second half of the 17th century, and then continued on until the 18th century. While many historians ignore any connection, Jane Caputi (1978) has shown that this spread was fostered by the invention of the printing press. Foreshadowing the 20th century Holocaust, the escalation of technology and of persecution goose-stepped together in a "march of progress".

Like the Holocaust, witch-hunting was justified by a need to "purify" society. This effort of purification focuses predominantly on deviant or defiant women who had rejected marriage as spinsters or who had survived it as widows. Women whose physical, economic, moral and spiritual independence and activities were perceived as threatening and were also targeted for torture and death by fire (Daly 1978).

This fear of witches has deep roots in an association of woman with wild uncontrollable nature. Witches came to symbolize the violent irrationality of nature, which raised storms, caused illnesses, destroyed crops, obstructed generation and killed progeny. Irrational woman, like chaotic nature needed to be controlled. Not only were deviant and wise women deemed evil but also those who were "melancholic". This melancholia is described as a depressed state characterized occasionally by threatening statements and odd behavior. Any woman can recognize something familiar and frightening in this description (Merchant 1980).

I asked our women if any shadow of witchcraft and charges of sorcery remains a reality for those who resource themselves through a direct connection to the natural world. Did they feel haunted by a fear that there is something "witchy" about that connection?

The first woman that I asked had difficulty discerning between shamanic practices and witchcraft. "I had a lot of distrust about what Maria was doing. I had to stay separate from what she was operating. It was the spirits that she was working with basic witchcraft rituals. That made my skin crawl and I don't want any part of it."
Another expressed a similar feeling. "I didn't like that witchy stuff that Maria was doing. I think that it was wrong."

The strong emotional charge in both these women's responses was met by my equally strong desire to minimize the issue. Surely, I reasoned, in. this modem day and age fear of witches is not a serious concern. In time, I remembered the pain of having one of my closest male colleagues, who had apparently been ingesting a fair amount of hallucinogenic substances, accuse me of sending a plague of rats into his house. And then I remembered another male colleague, presumably sober, telling me that he had been having strange psychic experiences and politely asking me if I was causing them. While both incidents were hurtful, it was also frightening to be accused of something that I couldn't prove that I didn't do.

I decided that the subject was worth pursuing and continued to interview participants, asking if they had any particular concerns about witchcraft and if they had ever been accused of that. My experience, it seems was not all that unusual.

"Accused? I would say more that it's just that people *assume* that I am a witch. Why? Because I am a woman alone and I have all of these rocks and feathers, shells and beads, and Native American masks all over the house. I just tell them that I am not a witch. And, yes, there is some fear there.

At the retreat we were reluctant to drum, and rattle and sing lest the forest service would hear us. I felt uneasy around the fire ... some kind of primal fear. Who is the leak? Who was the Spook? Who was going to turn us in, collect information to use against us? Irrational maybe, but I definitely felt it."

For some it brought up issues from childhood. "Actually, my family called me 'The Witch' when I was growing up. They couldn't tolerate my ugly, bitchy, angry side. I think what was meant was 'bitch' but they did use the word *witch.* like I was some force of nature poisoning everything." Nowadays I do experience women's spirituality groups that emphasize ritual as frightening. Something about the drama of being public about woman power ... I am afraid, maybe, that I would like it too much. There is a level of excitement about it that is too much, too much charge ... maybe a fear that participating would blow my cover, of being found out. It's a gross cellular sort of fear that I will lose friends, family and that I will lose professional standing and be run out of town.

Being outdoors with grounded women whose strong connection is personal and well integrated is OK That feels really good to me....Issues from adolescence also surfaced.

"Interesting, yes, I recognize the fear and concern there. And, yes, I was accused in high-school. I had a friend who said she was a witch, she was lighting white candles or something. Another friend of mine just flipped out that I was friends with this person and accused me of being a witch too. Guilt by association. It scared me. Now, I am much more relaxed about all that. Healing ritual practices seem very natural to me. This is a good reminder to not forget about the old days when anything about women and nature was witchcraft."

Acknowledging the seriousness of the issue for her, this woman tried to deflect the fear with humor. "Accused of witchcraft? Oh yes! I make flower essences from my garden. I try to counter the charge with lightness and humor. I have a bumper sticker that says, 'My other car is a broom!'"

Other women, however, didn't feel any particular charge around the issue. Combing through the interviews again, I noticed that those of us who had the most fear of accusation were the most identified as alternative healers and health professionals and that several of us had been nurses and midwives. It didn't seem surprising, therefore, that traces of fear remain in the aftermath of historical persecutions.

Catching a whiff of burning pine, I looked across the flames at my friend Maria, gazing thoughtfully into the night. This gentle, light-hearted woman of leonine grace and great spiritual depth embodies generations of shamanic wisdom. By certain fundamentalist standards, even in today's culture, she would be regarded as a "witch". Fear of accusation was with us that night as a necessary component to healing the wounded feminine. And then, my attention was drawn to a tangle of torn spider webs in a pile of nearby firewood. Patience, I thought; and of Adrienne Rich's poem *Natural Resources* (1978):

This is what I am: watching the spider Rebuild-
patiently, they say
But I recognize in her
Impatience -my own
The passion to make and make again
Where such unmaking reigns.

Grieving with the Enemy, Russia and the Tragedy of War

Only the dead have seen the end of war.

Plato

Soon after our return from our Moon Rock retreat an invitation arrived to continue participation in an ongoing Russian-American exchange program coordinated by Valery Mikhailovich Mikhailovsky M.D. As Russia's leading trauma specialist, Valery founded a clinic specializing in post-traumatic stress education and recovery, with special emphasis on combat and other war-related traumas. His clinic also has programs for handicapped children, adults and their families. Cliff Waterson and the Mountain Air Vietnam Veterans had been with him in Russia over the summer. Together, they focused on the shared issues of soldiers returning from Vietnam and Afghanistan, veterans of an unpopular war, returning to an uncomprehending homeland. Now, Valery stated, he wanted to turn his attention toward the issues of traumatized women.

This invitation to Russia was offered in the hope that we could under- take and develop some sort of new model for cross-cultural trauma work. A need for a new model was clearly expressed in a follow up letter from Elena Cherepanova, head of the Society of Psychological Stress in Moscow and chair of the Belarussian Research Institute for Education. Her invitation to present an innovative model for social trauma work clearly reflected a sense of overwhelm:

"With the frequency of disasters, wars, national conflicts and violence on the increase all over the world, treatment is often a question of real physical, social, cultural and political survival for the involved region. Professionally trained people are in short supply, and it is imperative that ways be found to train not only mental health professionals but local, non-professional volunteers, as well."

Her letter communicated a profound understanding that trauma is a global issue and that there is an urgent need to develop international, cross-cultural, cost-effective trauma education and recovery programs based upon easily transmitted concepts.

At the time, Russia seemed to be a logical choice for a place to undertake the development of new models for social trauma education and recovery. The need was clear, and also widely understood by both professionals and non-professionals. Russian people were well aware that one couldn't always rely on a health care system to help them. Moreover, there was not time, money, facilities or trained people to do individual psychotherapy or to be able to use that as a model for treatment. And then, there was the reality: *vast* numbers of people in need of care. *Vast* numbers of people,

Cliff had emphasized at our first meeting, and, yes, here it was, a challenge to at least begin to recognize and address this *vastness* in the realm of social trauma. Russia then was on the edge of all out civil war, with fear and hatred fostering forces of extreme nationalism and bitter ethnic conflicts. Boris Yeltsin's Russian Federation inherited an ecological disaster. Every major river in Russia is polluted, and 35 million people live in cities where it is dangerous to breathe the air. Russian officials attribute the precarious health of their nation's young people, only a quarter of whom are healthy, to air and water pollution. Life expectancy for elderly people ranks below the lowest in Europe (Fesbach a. Friendly 1992).

Generational trauma is a very real issue in Russia. In modern times alone, one can trace a legacy of trauma from the empire of the Tsars to World War I, the Russian Revolution, World War II and the insanity of Stalinist purges when 30 million people or more died or disappeared in labor camps, famines and mass deportations. Liquidation of millions of citizens helped shape a tragic future of repression, stifled enterprise, insularity and global aggression. Cold War, an arms race, the Afghanistan war and then a rapid dissolution of the former USSR (Talbott 1992, p. 32-69).

In addressing our task of creating a joint program, there were many questions. How can one promote healing in times of transition and absolute anarchy? *How* to care for people when systems break down, nothing works, and resources are unavailable and the future uncertain? And, of immediate concern, for me, was that this invitation was for October, just on the edge of Russian winter. Any work outside in nature would be limited, at best. How then to translate what I had learned about healing through the natural world into an indoor clinic situation? And, even more challenging was the question of how to work with traumatized people without a good command of Russian and a limited understanding of their culture.

In desperation, I called upon Darrell Sanchez, the most kinesthetic person that I have ever known. Darrell had been a student of mine and of Peter Levine in Boulder, Colorado and had gone on to develop his own very unique and kinesthetically oriented ways of working with trauma. We were both experienced in Rolfing and other body-oriented modalities, and in that sense, held a shared understanding of somatic communication. Trained also as a mime, Darrell's preferred mode of communication was non-verbal. He understood both my dilemma and also my desire to find a creative solution. And so, we began a series of explorations around kinesthetic, cross-cultural, non-verbal options for working with trauma, which continue to this day. I also returned to the University of California at Berkeley for intensive studies of Russian language and culture.

It soon transpired that whatever I was able to accomplish in this undertaking would never, ever, be anywhere close to barely enough. I flew non-stop from San Francisco to Moscow and was soon confronted at Sheremetyevo airport with the sharp sting of winter air. Winter, I came to understand, was always hard for Russia. The murderous violence of Russian winters, so deadly for invaders, has also provided a powerful catalyst for drastic change. With the onset of the cold, food is difficult to find and prices rise. The Romanov dynasty, Alexander Kerensky's provisional government and Mikhail Gorbachev's USSR, all came crashing down under the added weight of sub-zero temperatures (ibid.).

I scanned into the waiting hordes, cautiously breathing cold damp air heavy with diesel fumes. Quite suddenly, I recognized Valery's tousled mane of peppered gray somewhere in the midst of a dense and anxious crowd that had gathered just outside of customs. Dressed in US Army combat fatigues given to him by American veterans, he was accompanied by a pleasant young lady with closely cropped red hair, the exact shade of my own. In crisp British English, Nellia introduced herself as our interpreter. Since our California meeting, I had studied Russian and Valery had studied English, but communication was still far from fluent. I understood that

I was to be the guest of the Mikhailovsky family at their apartment in Zelenograd. And then, Nellia quickly disappeared. "I have a date," she explained, in a note of sprightly grievance, "and you must never keep a Russian man waiting" Explanations for this reasoning were long in coming.

Zelenograd is an electronic and technological center, a kind of Russian version of Silicon Valley. The town, less than thirty years old, was built near an area devastated by heavy fighting during the German invasion of 1941. A number of war memorials to Russian warriors who fell in that struggle are found throughout the city and along modem roadways. Their largest monument, perpetually decorated with red flowers, marks that absolute boundary where German military forces could advance no further. Until recently, Zelenograd was off-limits to foreigners because of the technological research done there that contributed to the Soviet space program.

We arrived at the family apartment as Valery's patient wife Liana, also a medical doctor, and their children were watching an Indiana Jones adventure movie. Gesturing toward the screen, Valery said, "I hope you like adventure. Everything in Russia is an adventure ... One challenge after another, and then another." This day's challenge was well underway for this family. They were in the process of moving out of their bedroom into the living room in order to offer me some degree of privacy. They would be quite comfortable, they insisted, explaining that there had been a time when four families had shared this two- bedroom flat. Valery's deep commitment to cross-cultural work had deep roots within his own family. His father was Jewish, one of the few survivors in his family after the 1941German invasion of The Ukraine. Valery's mother is Russian and his wife Muslim.

It took nearly two full days and nights to adjust to the time change, and I sank into long stretches of deep sleep before I could begin to take in the gray dawn of reality. Russia outside my grimy window appeared impenetrably bleak. A chorus of crows, hundreds of dark forms, whorled against a colorless sky. Slowly arriving in present time, I realized the extent of my fear, with limited ability to communicate, and completely dependent on people that I did not really know. There was no telephone and I had no idea how to escape, if that ever became necessary. Years later, the memory of that dark chorus of crows would return, in a long letter from Valery, after a time when I had come to understand much more about him, Russia and war.

As we prepared to leave the apartment for the clinic, Valery un- plugged his car battery from an electrical outlet in his kitchen. This was part of a daily ritual that required carrying this precious battery down seven floors and out into the parking area to rejoin the engine. This procedure reduced the risk that his car would be stolen and also served to extend the life ofhis battery, for batteries were a valuable commodity, in very short supply. A flat tire delayed our departure.

The director was the only person at his clinic who knew how to drive, and his own car was the only vehicle available. Sub-zero temperatures are hard on automobiles. Anti-freeze was not an option, and gas expensive and rationed. For one 30-minute trip to Moscow, Valery would often spend three hours in line waiting for half a tank of fuel, which would cost half a month's salary. He kept his English grammar books on the front seat next to him. "Gas line is my study time," he explained.

Patients and staff use public transportation. There were, however, no facilities for disabled people in the public transport systems. If people in wheelchairs want to come for treatment, Valery must begin early in the day to drive around to their various addresses, pick them up, sometimes literally, and assist them in getting into his car, secure their wheelchairs onto the luggage rack, drive them to the clinic and then assist them up a flight of stairs into the building. At the end of a day, the process is reversed and then, more time in the gasoline line.

We had sleet that morning, and the roads were slippery. Public roads were not maintained, and giant potholes forced vehicles headed in both directions to swerve in and out of any semblance of orderly lanes. Sheets of muddied ice water were splashed onto the windshield by oncoming and surrounding traffic, making visibility uncertain. Relatively at ease with nightmare road conditions, Valery began to tell about how he came to found his trauma center.

In 1983 he was serving as a pulmonary disease specialist at the Moscow Region Veterans Hospital located on the outskirts of Zelenograd. During that time, he headed a 60-bed pulmonary rehabilitation unit designed to serve older veterans of World War II as well as younger men who had served in Afghanistan. In working with these men he began to "intuit", as he described it, that the patients who had been in combat were showing signs of stress in those kinds of patterns which later came to be understood as post-traumatic stress disorder. The existing program in his unit was a strictly medical model with no provision for addressing the role of stress on mental and physical well being.

Valery decided that special programs needed to be designed for veterans who had experienced what is now known as "combat trauma". The hospital vigorously resisted this idea, but the veterans themselves recognized the need and joined him in lobbying for a special unit. As various veterans' organizations joined the effort, a great struggle ensued in an attempt to force medical and administrative authorities to address the effects of combat trauma. In Valery's mind, the need was so great, and the system so unresponsive, that a whole new model for treatment must be created. Psychotropic medications were not an option since they were, for the most part, unavailable.

Valery's new model stressed education and having each patient assume responsibility for overseeing his own recovery. He wanted to :find ways to help veterans move away from dependence on an inadequate system and :find ways to lead balanced lives of self-regulation. Using techniques of self-hypnosis and oriental balancing and martial arts techniques, he began teaching patients how to moderate their own stresses and move toward balance.

Valery and his staff taught the patients how to monitor their own vital signs, blood pressure, temperature and so forth, as well as how to change their own dressings. Patients were allowed and even encouraged to help each other with these procedures. The hospital administration was adamant that this unit must close. There were a series of professional and political battles that culminated in a hunger strike at the hospital where Valery, his staff and some of the patients were held during a long siege. At last, a compromise was agreed upon. Dr. Mikhailovsky and his staff would leave the hospital. The City of Zelenograd would give them a building and some funding to establish a Post-traumatic Stress recovery clinic.

Valery's sister Sophie Mikhailov, also a physician, joined the staff. Medicine had been a family affair for many generations of Mikhailovsky who practiced in the multi-ethnic former Soviet Republic of Dagestan. Brother and sister had years of experience working together with the Cosmonauts in the Russian Space program at

Startown. Eventually, the traumatic stress program expanded to include handicapped children and their families and was opened to anyone, without charge, who is suffering from any kind of trauma. Having the word International in the title of this International Center School of Rehabilitation was especially important, because they wanted to emphasize their understanding of trauma as an international issue, not just something that happens to Russians.

My arrival at the clinic began with warm greetings from Sergei Sakarov, a gentle handsome man whom I had met in America. A poet and a veteran of the war in Afghanistan, Sergei left his career as a mechanical engineer to become a massage therapist at The Center. He explained that most of the activity takes place in a large multi-purpose treatment room used for massage, and other forms of body and movement work. This space also serves as a meeting place for group and/or movement therapy with handicapped children and their parents, wounded war veterans, handicapped adults and grieving mothers whose sons were killed in Afghanistan. On any given day all of these activities may go on simultaneously. The Russian sense of boundaries and privacy is decidedly non-Western, and they strongly believe in the healing power of inclusiveness and community. They don't seem to find any particular value in separating categories of patients by age, gender or by the nature of their trauma.

I had expected that my first morning at the clinic would be spent in some sort of convivial conference exploring ways that we could work together to learn from each other and develop joint work. When I arrived with Valery and Nellia, the staff meeting was already in progress and Sophie, in an all-business mode, did not welcome the interruption. Eyes widening at the sight of me, she riffled through a few pages of a Russian language copy of my "Chinese Firecracker Syndrome" and slapped the rest onto to the table. "You," she said, "are not welcome here! We have no need whatsoever for your kind of therapeutic work and you should immediately go back to Vienna!" "I am not Chinese," she exclaimed, "and I have no interest in firecrackers!" Valery's visage was totally blank, and he said nothing. This was my first experience of what I came to term "Russian face". In stunned silence I withdrew along with my interpreter.

In time, Nellia was able to gain access to my offending paper and determine that our problem was one of mistranslation. My English title "The Chinese Firecracker Syndrome: A Developmental Analysis of Combat Trauma" had been translated into Russian as something like "A Psychoanalytic Analysis of Chinese Firecrackers". Sophie had, therefore, assumed that I was a Freudian psychoanalyst interested only in the symbolism of Chinese firecrackers. Quite understandably, Sophie felt that their seriously overextended Center needed a trauma specialist, and she was unwilling to waste any of her valuable time with such abstract Viennese and Oriental concepts. With this clarification, I was permitted to return to the meeting. For me, this lesson was well taken. More than ever, I understood the necessity for understanding enough of the written and spoken language of my host countries to be able to determine when I was being mistranslated. Seemingly innocent and rather simple mistranslations can easily lead to any number of cross-cultural upsets.

Much later, Valery explained the cultural necessity for his "Russian face". "This face," he explained, "we have learned to adapt under highly charged circumstances where the outcome is unknown." In time, I came to appreciate the value of this balanced presentation of a determinedly neutral visage.

Valery's older sister, alert and delicate as a wren, sat at the head of the conference table with her eleven-year-old son Andruska close by. Her boy was quietly working out a number of numerical puzzles. Born without legs, Andruska and children like him were not permitted to attend public schools. Later, over tea, around the samovar, Sophie explained that about 10 %of Russian children are born with deformities. Of the 9 million babies born that year, only 9% were entirely healthy. These birth defects, she continued, are the result of nuclear fallout, industrial pollution and various other factors. Later, for reasons of her own, she denied any recollection of our conversation. In Russia, I was to learn, this is not, at all, unusual.

Valery had mentioned that I had experience working with traumatized women, and Sophie wondered how I might do something like that at their clinic. The idea that women would want to be together in any kind of healing group was new to them, and they were curious. I suggested that Sophie and I arrange to meet with a group of women who had suffered traumatic leg amputation, mothers of handicapped children, along with some of the grieving mothers and any other women who may want to join us.

And so, our women's group met one morning from 10 until noon. We began slowly, as the idea of focusing on women's issues was new, and participants were unsure as to how to proceed. I explained that in America many women had found it easier to do some of their healing work in same-sex groups and that women had much to offer each other in terms of mutual understanding and support. I asked them if there had been women in their lives who had been particularly helpful or supportive of them. A conversation then began to emerge about the roles of their mothers, grandmothers and special women friends in their recovery process.

I wondered what kinds of issues they thought would be interesting or important to explore together. One woman asked for some tools in helping her cope with depression. The others quickly agreed that this was of great concern to them as well. Knowing that the clinic emphasizes self-care and self-regulation, I decided to focus on some of the non-psychological factors that may induce or worsen depressive feel- ings such as the importance of diet, that certain allergies can produce depressive reactions, along with certain medications, overuse of drugs and alcohol, and structural problems such as head injuries, a fall or blow to the sacrum, hormones, the importance of regular exercise, and so forth. We also explored a possible relationship between depression and creativity. Discussion was lively, and Sophie pronounced the event a success.

Word soon reached other staff members that the women's group had important information about depression. When we met the following morning, Andruska wheeled himself in to join us. Although surprised by his willingness to be there, I was touched by his openness and curiosity and could not bring myself to explain that this group was only for women.

In resuming our discussion from the previous morning, we were soon interrupted by Vladimir Shuleppin, a burly, wild-haired massage therapist who entered the room by a series of backward somersaults. One of the women spoke sharply to him, explaining that this group was "only for women." "But," he insisted, "that means that I can be here!" Vladimir had brought along his diploma as a registered *med-cistra* or "medical sister", which is a Russian term for registered nurse. Knowing that I was there to learn as well as to teach, I immediately recognized the authority of his diploma and invited him to join us.

Vladimir told us that he had pain and depression after a series of automobile accidents and that he believed that some of the low energy that he felt afterward was due to cranial compression along the base of his skull. Together, we showed the group various manipulative, corrective and self-care techniques that can release tension and pressure in the occipital area. Other male members of the staff soon appeared to join in the information exchange. Later, through Valery, the male members of the staff requested that they be included in my women's group. I immediately agreed. While the women were receptive to the idea of a women's group, the men were not, and they felt excluded. A main component of this community's survival strategy in these difficult times has been to work together in groups where no one is excluded. Gender work is clearly not a priority when daily survival is such an ongoing struggle.

This policy of inclusion is extended to the patients as well. Sophie explained that they make no hierarchical distinction between staff and patients. Many of the volunteer and paid staff members had originally come to the Center as patients. At this clinic the doctors cook and clean. Meals are prepared daily together with patients and staff Nellia explained that most Russian people don't have the money to eat in restaurants and that they are very distrustful of food prepared outside the home. There is no public health department inspecting and regulating the quality of food or kitchen facilities. Food is expensive and supplies precarious so it is necessary for both patients and staff to bring food from their gardens that they have dried or preserved to last through the long winter.

Warm cooked food is considered essential for the staff and their seriously ill patients who travel many hours in sub-zero weather on unreliable transportation to reach the clinic. Most people do not have telephones at home, so communication is erratic. All appointments, therefore, are always uncertain. On one particularly frustrating morning, none of the activities we had planned materialized due to a sudden snowstorm that had thrown public transport into a state of utter chaos. A stressful day, Valery observed, and a good time to leave for the forest. He is deeply convinced in the healing and restorative power of the natural world. His war veterans treatment program always includes what he calls "wild nature", or wilderness work.

The Center is also affiliated with Solsnitaya (Place of Sunshine), a beautiful rustic old style Russian retreat compound located in the nearby forest of Bolina. All of the wooden buildings there were designed by Anatoli Wassilovich Ryadinsky, who looked like a thoroughly wild and benevolent giant out of some Russian fairy tale. His extraordinarily unique, richly textured structures were hand built and elaborately carved without the aid of power tools. I could only marvel at the intricate sculpturing of the spiraling poles, beams and planks, which displayed a wide variety of traditional and contemporary Slavic patterns. Many had entrance way and window coverings hung with intricate webs of macramé rope. A series of these wooden cottages clustered around an open-hearth area equipped with long heavy chains designed to hold huge cast iron cauldrons of soups and stews.

Anatoli greeted us with the informal warmth of a generous bear hug. Sensing that I was unaccustomed to below freezing temperatures, he quickly began to build a fire and collect ingredients for a massive stew. The first order of business was selecting from a pile of potatoes those small enough to be cooked quickly under the ashes. Anatoli dug a hole under the fire and buried the "kartoskas". Following his directions, we began chopping tomatoes, carrots, onions and more potatoes. When English and

Russian proved insufficient we were able to communicate in German. Like many soldiers of the Red Army, Anatoli had been stationed in East Germany for a number of years and had a working knowledge of the language. During my graduate years at U. C. Berkeley only a reading knowledge of German was required, so my conversational skills were quite limited. Nevertheless, we managed.

Knowing that night would fall quickly on this already dark day, we set off for a brisk walk toward the shores of a nearby lake. I was riveted by the delicate, almost lacy quality of this Russian forest. Long veils of gray mist hung just above the water. Slanting rays of late afternoon sun cast the landscape in a mellow saffron light. Settling into this deep sensate realm of the natural world, I listened for the mysterious language of Russian earth, coming through trees, across water and emanating from the forest floor. Gunshots rang through the air. Valery had warned that there were hunters nearby. My mind, however, had been on the traumas of war and the sound of gunfire brought forth the recurring realization that there is no end in sight to the tragedy of armed conflict here or anywhere else.

I thought of modem Russia from the Empire of the Tsars to World War I, the Russian Revolution, World War II, the Stalin purges, when many millions died, disappeared into labor camps, famines and mass deportations. Liquidation of millions and millions of citizens helped shape a tragic future: repression stifled enterprise, insularity and global aggression. Cold War, the arms race, Star Wars, the Afghanistan war, and now the rapid dissolution of the former Soviet Union. Forces of extreme nationalism, bitter ethnic conflicts, fear and hatred were leading Russia toward a dangerous edge (ibid.).

Shots again. We are, I thought, hunters of a different kind. We are hunters in search of very important information. How, we want to know, (Cliff again), can one promote healing in times of transition and absolute anarchy? How to care for people when all the systems break down, nothing works, resources are unavailable and the future uncertain?

Darkness fell and a sudden wall of cold sent us back toward the comfort of the hearth. Our "kartoskas" were ready. We were hungry and grateful for the opportunity to ground the afternoon thoughts in the elemental flavors of wood, fire and earth. It was well after dark as Valery changed another flat tire on his overworked vehicle and we prepared to return to the Center. We were expecting a week-long visit from Hussein and "his children" coming to Moscow from Dagestan to participate in a major martial arts competition.

Relative Balance in an Unstable World

Hussein has been an important teacher for The International Center School of Rehabilitation. Born with congenital heart problems, his physical activities were severely limited during his childhood. Im- patient with this situation, Hussein trained himself in physical and meditative balancing techniques that eventually allowed him to assume a normal life. As an adult, he trained at the Peking Academy of Martial Arts where he graduated with the highest honors. Hussein maintains a Wu Shu (martial arts) training center called, The Five Directions which is located in the mountainous region of Dagestan, situated at the junction of the European and Asian continents. This primarily muslim area is noted for its ethnic diversity. While the common language is Russian, there are 32 ethnic groups in the region that speak over 40 languages and dialects. The International Center School is committed to the idea of strength in diversity and is dedicated to the ongoing use of cross-cultural healing methods.

The next morning, we arrived at a nearby gymnasium for the competition. Hussein's team, ranging in age from 7 to 13, performed well. The overall scores for the team, however, were disappointing. Vladimir Ivasin, one of their teachers, explained that the Russian judges were prejudiced against the Dagastani team "because of the war." We had heard daily rumors of civil war in the Caucasus. Sporting events were not immune from political pressure – a difficult lesson for children.

During Hussein's visit, I learned that, in his decidedly non-western approach to post-traumatic stress responses, he avoids the notion of psychopathology, believing that these kinds of overwhelming life events could happen to anybody. For purposes of education, Hussein approaches PTSD responses as "imbalances". The recovery program , that he helped to formulate invites one to consider that human beings are not necessarily always balanced. The task, rather, is to learn the ways that one can get knocked off balance and then to learn the skills to rebalance.

Balance is presented as an ability to function within a particular range of energy, not too much, not too little. Through ancient oriental practices, physical, mental and spiritual faculties are all engaged. While attention to various aspects of practice waxes and wanes, there remains a connectedness, a continuum, throughout the experience. Resources of the whole being are tapped, and one has a bit of practice of being whole.

Later that evening I had the opportunity to observe Hussein work- ing with patients. On this occasion, he was working with three young women who had lost their legs in accidents. "Turning one's attention inward," he says, "is a powerful agent for change." A specialist in sword form Tai

Chi, Hussein is very much the gentle warrior. He was teaching the young women the art of maneuvering long wooden poles to aid in stretching their muscles to promote length and flexibility, all the while attending to the issue of physical confidence.

One of the women sought his advice about panic. "I get so frightened sometimes ... half of my body is gone. In unfamiliar situations if someone is rude or jostles me, I feel that I cannot defend myself ... I start to panic." Hussein understood. "Begin with your breath," he told her. "When everything feels out of control ... attend to your breathing... THAT you can control." He showed her how to focus on her exhale and breathe out slowly. He then instructed her to resist the urge to inhale rapidly ... and stay with a series of slow, deep, out breaths. "If you allow the panic in your breath, you will lose power and focus. Stay balanced with your breath. This will increase your options and your ability to find other resources." The idea of breath as a path to balance and a source of strength was new to her. Exhaling, she thanked him and the lesson continued.

Later, Hussein's children convened in the special events room to demonstrate their considerable mastery of Wu Shu. In observing their great capacity for flexibility and focus, I thought of the wars brewing in the Caucasus, not all that far from Dagestan. Good preparation, I thought, for growing up in a time of cultural and historical upheaval. *RELATIVE* balance, I thought, is what is important, Hussein emphasized. "Nothing is ever really stable. Humans live in an ever-changing environment. Earth herself is always in motion."

I understood the principles of relative balance from my experiences in the natural world at Mountain Air and Moon Rock. In Boulder, with Darrell Sanchez, I began to explore various ways to translate the les- sons of wilderness work, of using natural metaphors, healing broken connections and moving out of fixity into flow, into a clinical setting. Darrell's first suggestion was that I just sit on a Swiss ball. These balls are marketed as exercise training tools and are popular in some health and fitness centers. These balls also offer a powerful metaphor because they are the same shape as our Earth, and, as such, evoke a deeply felt sense of "home".

The simple act of sitting on one of these balls can introduce one to an experiential knowledge that we were mothered out of the substance of this planet and that her elements remain resonant with own. Three fourths of our bodily mass is fluid, and the chemical constituents of our blood resembles those of sea water. Life on Earth is a water-based system. The human nervous system is not designed to orient to a flat motionless surface. The deeper geophysical truth is that "home" is a fluid-moving sphere, which supports very subtle movements of shift- ing, tectonic plates floating on a molten core of fire and metal. It should not be surprising that sitting on the ball would evoke a felt sense of fluid connection to this water planet when one considers that the world views of shamanic traditions, Asians cultures and of Western philosophy, up until the time of Descartes, were permeated with this kind of thinking. In the Tao Te Ching, for example, we read "Mankind follows the way of the Earth. The earth follows the way of the Tao and the Tao follows the ways of Nature. The human being, Earth and the cosmos are modeled on each other. They *correspond."* A felt sense of this fundamental reality can be an important intervention in states of broken connections and traumatic fixity.

During our explorations, Darrell and I found that the subtle motions of these balls could facilitate deep and subtle awareness states that relate to postural, proprioceptive and vestibular reflexes within the autonomic nervous system. We observed that sitting on the balls would precipitate spontaneous movements, and in some instances, deep states of postural meditation would also arise. Used in this way, we found that the balls can provide an important kinesthetic, non-verbal resource for accessing traumatic fixation.

We found that when someone sits very still on the ball with their eyes closed there is an almost immediate tendency to become disoriented and then begin accessing postural and orienting reflexes. Depending on the degree and level of trauma in the nervous system, the person would then exert physiologic and physical effort to orient in space while remaining on the ball. This kind of trauma work needs to be done with great care because of the speed with which it can produce an arousal in the autonomic system. However, when done with careful attention to pacing and context, this kind of exercise can provide an important step in retraining lost postural and orienting reflexes. The ball can also be very effective in retraining a person's falling reflexes. The safety of the ball in these exercises resides in the fact that the ball is very receptive to weight, feels comfortable and playful, with the body not far above the floor.

In the wake of Hussein's visit, Valery invited me to introduce my developing version of the relative balance work, using Swiss balls. We agreed to begin with the three young women who had lost their legs in accidents. Without any form of introduction we placed the balls in the treatment room before the women arrived. We then assumed the role of observers who did not assist or interfere with their process. When the women entered the area in wheelchairs, they nodded greetings in our direction and then immediately moved toward the balls.

Clearly, the impulse was to try to find ways to move onto them and balance.

It took the women less than one day to learn to balance without assistance. Balancing on the ball was accomplished primarily through the pelvic floor, since relying on legs was not an option. As the pelvic floor responded to the softness and support of the moving sphere, there came a sense of finding ground somewhere other than through their legs. This produced a profound sense of relief, renewed confidence and increased option. Their success in this endeavor confirmed my observations at Moon Rock that one can ground through the pelvic floor and that one does not have to have legs in order to find a grounded connection to the earth.

On the second day, the women entered the treatment room and positioned themselves on the balls. "Let's dance!" they said. Valery began playing audiotapes of rock music and these women evolved an exciting new art form which they called *"ball* room dancing". In a discussion group afterward, the women expressed their feelings of liberation while moving on the balls. It gave them, they said, the kind of freedom to move that they had only experienced while in water. There were logistical problems in getting to the water, however, and it was much easier just to move onto a ball. Even water, they agreed, restricted their movements by slowing them down, and while on the balls they could also move freely in the air.

Up until this time none of the women had been willing to discuss the circumstances surrounding their accidents. While Valery felt that they were still not ready to do that, he noticed a substantial gain in their sense of physical confidence. As this confidence increased he noted a shift in their willingness to at least begin to discuss some of the emotional and logistical difficulties that resulted from their accidents, with each other and with the staff.

The work with the Swiss balls opened new directions for working with people who had undergone trauma and were left feeling un- grounded and without a sense of confidence, stability and "response ability" in their lower structures. This pattern is often found in those who have suffered overwhelming experiences in the pelvic area such as sexual abuse, childbirth and invasive medical procedures. Part of the survival strategy for undergoing unwanted sensation in the pelvic region often seems to be a kind of neuromuscular response which results in pulling the sensate awareness up above the diaphragm or even all the way up into the neck If awareness is permanently withdrawn from the lower body, this can impair the felt senses in way that bodily responses to threat are impaired. Thus, a cycle of re-traumatization may be set into motion.

In stage-related recovery, it also became clear, over time, that to begin grounding work in a standing position may be too overwhelming for those who have lost confidence in their lower structures. Focusing on bodily awareness in this position can bring up a sense of vulnerability, anxiety and powerlessness in the lower body and also a level of activation that feels overwhelming. As part of the process of building resources for someone who has lost a sense of confidence in their lower limbs, working with the ball in a sitting position can provide a less activating option. Pleased with the early explorations of the relative balance work with balls, I faxed an enthusiastic note to Darrell. In time came the reply that he was now turning his attention to trauma work with relative bal- ance in a standing position. The results of his next level of exploration also turned out to provide valuable non-verbal options for traumatic amputees as well as many other kinds of trauma.

Body-oriented trauma work was an essential component of the overall treatment strategy at the Center. Valery believes that people can be seriously weakened by feelings of helplessness. Confidence in one's ability to mobilize one's own resources is itself a powerful agent for change. An essential factor in resourcing trauma survivors, he maintains, lies in understanding the psychophysiological or "body mind" components to the experience of trauma. The *samsa regulatsi* or self-regulation techniques taught to his patients are based upon the belief that disease and trauma, in particular, are related to a breakdown in the immune system. The question which arises is whether the control mechanism for the immunological is beyond the reach of human intelligence or whether it operates entirely within the autonomic nervous system.

In Russia, a series of investigations by K. M. Bykov began in 1924 demonstrating that the ANS is only *relatively* autonomic and is subject to voluntary control Bykov and his associates worked with Pavlov's theories of conditioned responses. Their studies indicated that if a process can be conditioned, then it is a modifiable process, and if autonomic processes can be conditioned, then they are not really autonomic at all (Bykov 1957).

Bykov's work made significant progress in bridging the gap between *psyche* and *soma* and there have been many other sources of evidence on the potential for internal self-regulation. In recent decades, the concept of the human brain has expanded far beyond that of an or- gan producing thoughts and memories. Harvard physiologist Richard Bergland developed the concept of the brain as the most prolific gland in the body. While the full inventory of the hundreds of secretions has yet to be completed, it is known that the brain produces encephalins and endorphins, which moderate pain and help set the stage for recovery (Ornstein 1986).

The brain has a role in the production of gamma globulin, vital to the immune system. The brain also produces interferon, which can serve as a potent anticancer agent. The vast array of substances produced by the brain are all connected to human development, fulfilling potential, the maintenance of health and defense against disease. The most significant factor in this process is that the secretions of the brain can be stimulated or diminished by thought, behavior or environment (ibid.).

Russian physician Boris Pasternak knew this to be true from his own empirical observations: "Your health is bound to be affected if day after day, you say the opposite of what you feel, if you grovel before what you dislike and rejoice at what brings you nothing but misfortune. Our nervous system isn't just fiction; it's part of our physical bodies, and our soul exists ... inside us ... it cannot be forever violated with impunity." (Dr. *Zhivago)*

It seems clear that techniques such as *samsa regulatsi* would be of tremendous value in totalitarian, or other repressive societies, or life situations, if one could learn to control at least one aspect of his own inner life. During these discussions with Valery, I thought of Norman Cousin's *Human Options* (1981) in which he defined the ability of the brain to perceive itself as its most spectacular achievement. By the very act of comprehending itself, the brain is enhanced and augmented. Knowledge becomes evolution and evolution becomes knowledge. For me however, the grim realities of social trauma present serious challenge to this degree of optimism.

We spent a day in Moscow visiting with Elena Cherepanova and other members of the Society of Psychological Stress in Moscow. It was clear that these solid unpretentious professionals were all experiencing an enormous sense of overwhelm. The topic that day, as it had been on many other occasions was the ongoing aftermath of the world's worst nuclear civil disaster at Chernobyl when the area was still part of the former USSR. On April25, 1986 an experiment went terribly wrong, causing the fourth reactor to melt down and explode. A volcanic release of highly radioactive uranium and graphite were expelled into the atmosphere, radiation 300 times greater than the bombing of Hiroshima, resulting in an international ecological calamity. We learned that more than 40o,ooo people had been evacuated from "the Zone", a 30-kilometer circle of highly radioactive terrain around the entombed reactor, creating a huge population of "environmental refugees". An unusually intense round of forest fires, over the course of the following summer, served to further the spread of radioactive particles. Troubling, as well, was the reality that another 4 million continue to live under conditions of severe radiological contamination. Not surprisingly, mental health specialists report an all-pervasive sense of depression and "victim mentality" throughout the region.

An unidentified number of men were recruited or conscripted for work as "Liquidators" for the cleanup at the reactor and the surrounding area. Of the 800,000 men registered, at least 2,000 have died. Twenty percent of these men committed suicide, and another 70,000 remain permanently disabled. While comprehensive assessment of the health effects remains incomplete, the anecdotal information that does exist is terrifying.

According to an article in the *Times* of London, "hospitals in Ukraine, Belarus and adjacent provinces are filled with victims. Entire wards are lined with gaunt, dying children. It is believed that an additional 800,000 children are at risk of contracting leukemia. Ukrainian doctors are now referring to what they call Chernobyl AIDS; an incurable radiation induced immune deficiency that is not understood. Also, there is well-founded concern that 90% of the local gene pool has been contaminated (Carothers 1991, pp.8-13).

Much about this disaster is new and unexpected. There just hasn't been a radiological accident on this scale before. And, I learned that it is far from over. Much of the damage that radioactivity causes to living cells manifests itself long after exposure. Tumors and leukemia may show up after three or four years, or longer, as well as genetically determined disorders that appear in succeeding generations (ibid.).

Desperately seeking any sort of inner and outer balance, I turned inward toward the thoughts of William Irwin Thompson: "The conscious purpose of science is control of Nature; its unconscious effect is disruption and chaos. The emergence of scientific culture stimulates the destruction on nature, of the biosphere of relationships among plants, animals, and humans that we have called 'Nature'.

The creation of a scientific culture requires the creation of a scientific nature, but since much of science's activities are unconscious, unrecognizedly irrational, and superstitious; the nature that science summons into being is one of abstract system and concrete chaos, e. g. the world of nuclear power and weapons. The more chaos there is, the more science holds on to abstract systems of control, and the more chaos is engendered. There is no way out of this closed loop through simple rationality, or through the governing systems that derive from the rationalization of society" (Thompson ibid.).

We were told that there is a widespread fear and mistrust of authority in the contaminated regions. Stress was now a major health problem in "The Zone". Thousands of children from the area had been suddenly separated from their families and sent to clinics in East Germany and Cuba for medical testing and evaluation. Many were gone for many months and then had the additional stress of re-adjusting to their families still living in the contaminated regions. The Chernobyl reactor and others like it were still in operation. All of those present at this painfully difficult meeting felt that the dangers of this kind of nuclear disaster were far from over. There remains the threat posed by 19 similar graphite-moderated reactors, time bombs that none of the now-independent republics can afford to shut down. Rumors persist that several of these fledgling republics, in desperate need of cash, are trying to play politics with the control of nuclear materials and are making separate deals with those we have come to understand as "rogue nations".

In the former USSR, it would appear that no one was willing to publicly acknowledge any of those grim graphic portents that appeared in 1957. A devastating nuclear waste explosion and the subsequent dumping of contaminated materials near Chelyabinsk, 900 miles east of Moscow, is now thought to have unleashed a deadly wave of pollution totaling about 1.2 billion curies, a unit measure of radioactive contamination comparable with the mere 3 billion curies from bombs released over Hiroshima and Nagasaki.

Albert Einstein left this life long before Chernobyl; nevertheless, he saw the "handwriting on the wall'. In a telegram sent on May 24th, 1946 Einstein said, "The splitting of the atom has changed everything except our way of thinking, and thus, we drift towards unparalleled catastrophe." (www.wit.com; Fesbach a. Friendly 1992)

Afghan Nightmare

"It's time, friend, time! For peace, the spirit aches."
Alexander Pushkin, 1834

During the latter part of my stay, I was invited to a ceremony honoring soldiers from Zelenograd who had been killed in the Afghanistan War. A central focus of this occasion was to be an unveiling of a memorial that was placed next to a monument honoring soldiers killed in their Great Patriotic War (World War II). Both memorials stood on a gentle incline just outside the gates of a local cemetery. The stark simplicity of both monuments serves to mark a grim reality of sacrifice and war.

The ceremony began on a relentlessly gray October morning. This funerary landscape was especially somber beneath leaden skies, sub- freezing temperatures and ground covered with scattered remains of a recent snowfall. Icy crystals of sleet stung my cheeks as I sought to find my place amongst a gathering of townspeople. The atmosphere was thick with melancholia. Growing numb with cold and an aching sense of tragedy, I watched and listened as various members of this community spoke of personal and social tragedies of war. The mayor spoke along with a representative of Veterans of the Great Patriotic War. Two mothers who had lost their sons in Afghanistan spoke at length of the depth of their sorrow at losing their children. My knowledge of Russian is very basic, but a mother's grief is universal, and I felt no need for translation.

Their ceremony concluded after a short speech by an Afghani veteran, followed by a poem read by another veteran and then a series of songs sung by a young veterans singing group. A memorial was unveiled, and people were invited to approach the monument with their prayers, memories, flowers and other offerings. Slowly, people began to approach the commemorative stone. Some were carrying candles burning in small glass containers, as well as photographs of young soldiers who had lost their lives. This ceremonial scene looked strangely familiar to me as I remembered Memorial and Veterans Day ceremonies of my childhood. They included speeches by the mayor, I now recalled, as well as representatives of local veterans groups, a song or a poem, a ceremonial placing of wreaths by the Gold Star Mothers who had lost sons in World War II and Korea.

Here it was, all again, on another side of our world. Another generation. Another war. Strange to be grieving all of this among these Russian people who, together with the Red Chinese, had been our enemies during my childhood and adolescence. Grieving with "The Enemy" brings this universal tragedy of war into painfully sharp focus. Regardless of who wins, our losses are staggering.

My face now wet with tears and snow; I felt the pain of freezing temperatures along with a senselessness and universality of suffering caused by war, to soldiers, their loved ones, families, friends and com- munity. I scanned the crowd for some, almost any, solace in familiar faces. They were not difficult to spot, as some of the Afghani veterans that I had met at Mountain Air were wearing American army combat fatigues given them by our local veterans' organization during their cultural exchange.

Many American veterans of the Vietnam War (1964-1973) and Russian veterans of Afghanistan find commonality in their experience of having participated in an unpopular war. The Red Army invaded Afghanistan on December 7, 1979. Nine years later, they withdrew with estimated casualties ranging from 15,000 to 39,000 dead. The present count of missing and unaccounted for soldiers rests uneasily somewhere around 320. Like our American army, the Soviet military was a multi-ethnic fighting force. Also, like the Americans in Vietnam, the Russians found themselves, as professionally trained soldiers, in a losing battle with raw unprepared local militia. This stress of war was further compounded by an inability to distinguish between civilians and combatants. Returning veterans from Afghanistan and Vietnam also shared an experience of returning to an uncomprehending society, which was both unwilling and unable to recognize post-traumatic stress responses and disorders as an aftermath of war. Both Russian and American soldiers knew the experience of being blamed for the losses suffered by their countries (Tamarov 1992).

After this ceremony, I began greeting Afghansi veterans that I had met in America. They, in turn, introduced me to the grieving mothers who had spoken that morning. I told them that although I barely understood Russian, I had deeply felt the import of their message. They urged me to join a banquet that was being held in a nearby civic facility, and I gladly accepted their invitation.

This banquet was held in a spacious hall located less than five minutes from the cemetery. Two rectangular tables were arranged with one horizontal table between to serve as the head table honoring mothers whose sons had been killed. White cloths draped tables set with pitchers of apple juice, together with bottles of wine and vodka. A first course soon arrived of potato salad, pickles and other savories, followed by pot roast with boiled potatoes. Dessert was chocolate and cream-filled pastries.

Food was scarce, prices high and lines long. Russia was undergoing a painfully difficult transition, and this memorial menu clearly reflected the importance that this community attached to this occasion. Our meal began with a toast from one of the mothers who had undertaken many of the logistical and organizational tasks involved in bringing this event to its present form. She expressed gratitude to all of those who had been of service and invited all participants to enjoy their food. As people began to eat, a local official stood up to offer a toast and began talking about how hard this war had been on parents and families. He then went on to address the chaotic and difficult times. "Why?" he demanded, "do our lives have to be so hard?" He emphasized that with a recent outbreak of civil wars within the former USSR, "Russians must not make war on other Russians!"

A group of Afghansi veterans gathered along one of the long back tables were drinking heavily and becoming increasingly restless. While some 9000 soldiers were killed during their 10 year occupation of Afghanistan, some 30 thousand, or more, Russians die of alcohol poisoning every year. The annual consumption of alcohol for Russia is higher than anywhere else on our planet (almost four gallons per capita, and almost half of that is vodka) (Time Magazine, Dec. 1992).

Suddenly, one young man stood up, interrupted the official and demanded that he and his friends be given time to recite each of the names of fallen comrades. The older man sat down. These recitations went on for a few minutes until they were interrupted by one of the mothers who rose to her feet. This mother firmly reminded them that this gathering was in honor of all of those killed in Afghanistan and individual naming was not appropriate at this time. The veterans group sat down as this woman silently held her vodka aloft in the gesture of a toast. Among the veterans of Afghanistan and their associates, a third toast is traditionally silent and in memory of those soldiers who did not return.

Almost immediately, another mother rose. This woman who had lost both of her sons in the war sharply reminded the restless veterans that while they did indeed need to remember their dead, they also needed to honor living, grieving families whose lives must go on. "Do not forget *us,"* she admonished. "Mothers without our sons. When I look at you, I am always looking for any of you that may have known my boys and might be willing to talk to me about them. We are still mothers. We still need sons. You are all our sons and we are your mothers!"

Mother Russia. Mother of Sorrows. These fierce women in black silks, shawls, and carefully mended lace brought to mind Joanna Hubb's *Mother Russia.* This sensitive contribution to Slavic studies draws close links between Russia's singularly powerful maternal archetypes and the misogyny of the Orthodox Church. Byzantine Christianity may have been more repressive of women than Roman Catholicism, she speculates, because their region was more vulnerable to the goddess-centered fertility religions of the Near East, and the Orthodox Church had to contend with unusually powerful matriarchal patterns (Hubbs 1988; see also Gray 1990).

Scholars concur that Russia is a region wherein female-centered cults and social orders lingered longer than in most other cultures. Early Slavic religion was strikingly deficient in dominant male deities. Worship of the Great Mother and other female deities common to agricultural societies prevailed long into the Christian era. Russian folklore remains especially rich in powerful female archetypes. *Polianitsy are* amazonian heroines of early Russian epics. The most fearsome and pervasive female prototype of all is *Baba Yaga,* a prescient old witch who has an aspect that can serve as a symbol of female wisdom at its most wrathful and punitive.

In few other countries, historians have noted, did women retain power so long over tribal institutions and maintain so forceful a role in family life. The heroes of Russian epics had to obey the orders of their mothers or wives, rather than those of male authorities. Contrary to Latin or Anglo- Saxon custom, a son needed his mother's rather than his father's blessing when he left home for war or any other quest for success and honor. To this day, few idioms so forcefully express a country's umbilical spell upon her people as the language of "Mother Russia". Several of the national rivers and the Volga in particular, are referred to as *Matrusuka,* "Dear Mother", while the very noun for "native land" is *rodina* from the word *rod,* which means "birth" (ibid.).

After the mothers had spoken, the room was quiet, and the young veterans left together for a smoking break. I visited with each of the mothers, who in turn, showed me pictures of their sons. The faces in those pictures looked so young. Many had been sent to Afghanistan at the age of sixteen, seventeen or eighteen. I showed them a picture of my father who had died at the age of twenty-five. Without the aid of translation, it was clear that we could agree that war held ongoing and devastating consequences for families.

As dessert and tea arrived, the veterans returned to the dining area. A young man with a guitar, who had sung at the unveiling ceremony, led his group toward the mothers. He was wearing US Army combat fatigues with Red Army medals pinned to his jacket. Nellia explained that he had suffered many head injuries, therefore, his eyes were un-even and unable to focus. Slowly the soldiers brought their chairs along toward the head table and sat facing the mothers. Gently, slowly, they began singing songs about the Afghanistan War ...The loneliness of the soldiers, days of boredom and fear, feeling crazy, lost and angry, and believing that no one that they loved could ever, ever, understand.

Gradually, some of these young men moved around to the other side of the head table, taking seats close to the mothers. The singing grew stronger as everyone drank, cried and shared their experiences in the aftermath of war. I was nearly overwhelmed by their compassion, pain, and recurring realization that there was absolutely no end in sight to this tragedy of war. Looking around this room, I was acutely aware of the fear and destructive nature of forces brewing within factions of extreme nationalism and bitter ethnic conflicts. There were bread lines in Armenia. Vast tracts of former Soviet territories were threatening to break from Moscow's rule. In trying to define their own nationhood, many Russians have not been willing to accept the idea that the l4 non-Russian republics of their fallen Soviet Union are now independent foreign countries.

The Russian army was threatening war in several of these republics. People are frightened by the Mafia and crime rates spiraling upward with inflation. Like most empires, it seemed clear that the physiognomy of Russia would continue to be molded by war and revolution. In *On Revolution* Hannah Arendt warned that wars easily turn into revolutions and that revolutions have shown an ominous inclination to unleash wars. The reason for this, she maintains, is that violence is a common denominator to both (Arendt 1973).

As word spread that the lady sitting with the mothers was American, I was soon surrounded by eager young men who struggled in English and in Russian to tell me that they were not my enemy. "Please, we do not want to fight with you. We are not your enemies. We were conscripted. We did not volunteer. We are so sorry." We held hands, and I looked into their faces and told them that I too was sorry and that I did not want our countries to fight.

As we were leaving, a deeply saddened older man approached us. He introduced himself as Vladamir Kuchrenkov, husband of Valentina, one of the mothers that I had been talking with. He explained that he was a widower and that she was a widow when they met at the cemetery visiting the graves of their sons. He carried a picture of his son and hers together in his wallet. After they married, they adopted a young girl from an orphanage. She was now thirteen and doing well in school, although he worried that she was so shy. They were glad to be parents again, he said, and they were trying to get on with their lives.

I gladly accepted an invitation to spend an evening with the mothers later on in the week. I told them that I had returned to the memorial the day after the ceremony to have a quiet visit with fewer people around. I noted that the Afghansi memorial was much smaller than the monument to the soldiers of the Great Patriotic War and seemed to be of a much more human scale. Standing before this black slab of highly polished granite one could see the names of the deceased engraved across one's own reflection.

Again, I thought of T. S. Eliot:

We die with the dying
See, they depart, and we go
with them We are born with
the dead
See, they return, and bring us with them
(Little Gidding: Four Quartets)

The memorial meant a lot to these grieving parents who raised funds for it themselves. Permission to erect this memorial was given after a long and difficult political and bureaucratic struggle. For a time, the Soviet government did not want to acknowledge that the tragic ordeal of Afghanistan was actually a war.

Throughout the evening, people spoke about their grief. Some parents never knew the circumstances of their sons' deaths. Others couldn't be certain that the bodies in the returning coffins were really those of their sons. "My son was 6'2", the coffin only 5' 11".

"Why? Maybe he is a prisoner somewhere. Maybe he is sick in some hospital ...What if he has lost his mind and is wandering in the desert."

These kinds of unanswered questions had haunted my family as well. My father was listed as missing in September, and the final telegram arrived nearly a month later. Desperately hopeful, the family continued to write to him. I remember reading these letters, alone in the old house, returned by the army after the war. A package of air mail envelopes stained with the dreaded splotch of back ink that signified "deceased" contained the last few letters that my grandmother wrote to her son in September and October of 1944-

"The telegram arrived from the war department telling Gwen (my mother) that you have been missing since September 21st. In spite of the risks and knowing the possibility of such a thing happening, it was nevertheless a shock to us all....But, I hope that you may be alive as a prisoner or hiding somewhere ... and we will continue to hope to hear from you eventually. ...You have no idea how much noise the clocks in the house make when things are quiet. There are times, now, when we just sit and stare without seeing each other ..."

In late October, final word came. Another year later, in October 1946, my grandmother received a letter from the War Department about her son stating that: "The records of this office disclose that his remains are interred in the US Military, St. Juan, plot B row 15178. This cemetery is located 17 miles northeast of Besancon, France. You may be assured that the identification and internment has been accomplished with fitting dignity and solemnity."

My grandmother was not at all reassured and immediately arranged to have her son re-interred next to his father in the family plot in the town where he grew up. My mother did not want to attend the graveside service. "How," she said, "do I know that it really is him in that coffin? Who knows where he is or what really happened to him?" Later, after my return from Russia, she was, reluctantly, somewhat able to share more of those ongoing fears.

While in Zelenograd, I asked people who had lost loved ones in Afghanistan, if they would be willing to speak about what kinds of things or experiences had helped, or would help, in coping with an overwhelming grief. "Information," was a frequent reply. Not knowing made resolution and acceptance even more difficult.

"Community" and "contact" were other frequent answers, as well as "being with others who share this kind of grief and who understand our feelings." Community, contact and information were often provided by return- ing veterans who were willing to visit the families of fallen comrades. Maintaining these relationships was an important component of com- munity healing, as was clearly evident at the banquet.

The "Red Star Mother's Association" wanted me to know, however, that for them, community, contact and information included a much larger issue. They found great comfort, they said, in communicating with other families outside of

Russia who understand the pain of war and who are also struggling to find ways to heal in a world which offers no end to the tragedy of war. "Do you know," they asked, "any family members, loved ones or veterans groups in America who are willing to communicate with us? If so, please give them our address."

The cross-cultural focus at the Center created an atmosphere especially conducive to international exchanges. Toward the end of this visit a luncheon meeting was held with a delegation of doctors from Communist China. China, I was reminded, is the only one of our world's great civilizations that still exists. The Chinese people have accomplished what the Babylonians, Greeks, Persians and Romans were unable to achieve. Through their own efforts, often at a terrible price, Chinese people have kept their country going and to this day it has remained whole (Dillard 1984). The men in this delegation ranged in age from their fifties to their seventies. Their generation would have witnessed, participated in and very likely sacrificed themselves for the "liberation of China." Their early lives would have been marked by civil war, world war and foreign occupation. Mao Tse Tung came to power in 1949. The Cultural Revolution, which lasted a decade (1966-1976), represented a culmination of a series of ruinous intervals of purgative campaigns.

The configuration of nationalities gathered around our table brought to mind the subject of enemies. Russia and China have a long history of animosity, and they were both important cultural enemies during my American childhood and adolescence. For my parents' generation, the enemies were the Germans and the Japanese. However, these Russian and Chinese "enemies" are my very own, specific to my generation. Many countries it would seem, change enemies with the generations and sometimes, more frequently.

"Enemies," the Dalai Lama says, "can be our greatest teachers" (Prevallet 1998). While the concept of "enemies as teachers" is spiritually complex, in the most straightforward sense, this has proven true in my life. The study of Chinese medicine and profound wisdom of my Chinese doctor Lam Kong have dramatically shifted my perspective on health and healing. And now, I am learning a great deal about Social Trauma from the Russians.

This day, the Chinese and their Russian hosts are wanting to learn from each other and their subject was "healing". Unspoken, yet pervasive in the atmosphere, was the question of whether Russia understood herself as part of Europe or Asia. Sophie served huge bowls of steaming borscht. No one spoke Chinese and so all other delegates had to communicate in Russian. The Chinese doctors spoke of great difficulties with problems of overpopulation. "As you know," they said, "we have too many people and not enough land. Here in Russia you have many open spaces in areas where there are harsh conditions. We are accustomed to harsh conditions. We will come and fill these open spaces." Around the table the Chinese saw only "Russian face". Valery reminded his Chinese guests that the subject was still and only "healing".

The Chinese delegates wanted to send five doctors to the Center. Valery agreed to only one. "No, "they said," we must send at least two, so that they will have each other for company." Valery said that while he understands their feeling, there is, as yet, no housing for two. As the meeting proceeded and it was agreed that the next step in the exchange will be with Valery traveling to China to study at their clinic at Xian. This, it turned out, was not be. The outbreak of civil wars in Russia's former republics was to draw Valery's attention in a very different direction.

My final day at the clinic was spent in deep conversation and conferences. We all agreed that the results of this exchange would become increasingly clear over time. I had traveled to Russia with specific questions about healing in times of transition and absolute anarchy. Cliff's question which had now become mine, as well, remained, "How to care for people when all the systems break down, nothing works, familiar resources are unavailable and the future decidedly uncertain?"

At the International School for Rehabilitation these questions were being addressed in a number of ways that seemed to be working well for them. They found a major strength in a commitment to community without great emphasis on hierarchy. The emphasis on balance and ' self-regulation, rather than psychopathology, appeared to be working ' well with many traumatized people. Educating patients to take charge of their own recovery process seems particularly important at a time when health care systems are unresponsive, breaking down or in a state of utter collapse.

I was deeply moved by the Center staff's ability to hold what might be called "a compassionate field of presence." In observing their work with patients it was clear that they had developed a great capacity to BE with whatever was happening, and allow each person's experience to BE whatever it was, or was not. Over and over, I witnessed a profound acceptance of the realities within the dark side of human nature. This was, however, a quality of acceptance, not resignation. This quality of acceptance provides a core of non-judgmental openness and attention that lays ground for a healing relationship.

On the morning of my departure I raced around packing and struggling with all sorts of unfinished details. Finally, together with the Mikhailovsky family, we observed a Russian ritual of sitting quietly together on the floor before departure. Nellia was available for last-minute communications. On the way to the airport, I asked her to finally tell me, why is it that she felt that Russian women must never keep a Russian man waiting? With a patient smile, she explained that, in Russia, at that time, there were many more available women than men. The majority of Russian men were ill, damaged from a war or alcoholic. "As a woman, if you are fortunate enough to have a man, you must do whatever it takes to keep him. If a man becomes displeased with you, he can easily turn to dozens of others. In Russia, you might say, men have what the Americans might call 'a seller's market'."

As we arrived at Moscow airport I prepared to begin a lengthy bureaucratic processes of passport control. Waiting for me there, I found the entire Center School staff and several volunteers who had come to see me off. Sophie brought the last of her winter apples. Other ladies had baked cookies and muffins so that I wouldn't be hungry on the plane. Sergei arrived in his US Army combat fatigues carrying a huge bouquet of pale gold chrysanthemums, the exact shade of my omnipresent parka. Gates closed behind me, and I began my journey through the bureaucratic maze. As I kept turning to look back toward them, they continued to wave, and no one left the gate until I boarded my flight 90 minutes later.

After take-off, an American stewardess spoke to me in Russian. Overwhelmed by this process of transition, I responded in English. "Oh," she said, "I am so sorry. I really thought that you were Russian." Reflecting upon this later, I slowly came to realize how deeply this exchange had impacted me in many more ways than I would ever have been able to imagine.

Relative Balance

"Somehow, myself survived the night- and entered with the day"

Emily Dickinson

My transition back to America was complicated and included a move from California to my rustic retreat of a St. Vrain River House, just outside of Boulder, Colorado. I was becoming a stranger to sleep and an absence of restorative rest was taking its toll. Still tired, I often rose during those chilly pre-dawn hours that had become that one part of my day that is truly private. Dawn begins long before sunrise, and those one or two hours before first light a appears became "my time", before daily pressures begin to consolidate. I was learning to enjoy this luxury of slowly emerging from a world of night and an always-mysterious realm of my unconscious.

I knew that I needed more transition time in an effort to balance he oscillating realities of my inner and outer worlds. Waiting for my morning kettle to boil, Runa Owlfeathers, my longhair calico tabby sat quietly on my desk. I found her at an animal shelter and was immediately drawn to those fierce golden eyes and widely spaced, tufted ears, which reminded me of a great homed owl. Mysterious creatures known as great homed owls have been seen as "cats with wings" and are often depicted as images of wisdom when seen with Athena, or as "screech owls of defiance" when they fly alongside Lilith, the exiled first wife of Adam. Owls are associated with healing, evil, fertility and death. This owl of a cat, I thought, would make an apt companion for plumbing those dark complexities of life and death that trauma work requires. On this dark morning, her clear gold animal gaze spoke of a consciousness shared - owls, cats and humans. We are all of us, she knows, both predator and prey.

Now, almost awake, I began that slow process of tuning into the soft glow of my computer screen. No news from Russia and this is not a surprise. More often than not, the Center's outdated computer and fax machine were bollixed up into some state of malfunction. Light appeared in and along the Eastern horizon, a soft gold slowly turned to a rosy glow revealing yet another day of clear blue sky. I knew that most of my Colorado winter would be taken up with adjusting to private practice and medical trauma work in a family practice clinic in Boulder.

I had come full circle now, a long way from inner city Baltimore, and was nevertheless returning to that familiar world of medicine, trauma, and the potential danger of my own sense of overwhelm. After settling in to my Boulder routine, I had a long conversation with Dr. Habibur Rahman, Chief of Protocol in the Ministry of Foreign Affairs in Afghanistan. My work with Russian veterans of their war in Afghanistan and their families was still on my mind. I was most inte- rested to hear about the war from the Afghan perspective. It was then 1993 and I had not considered the possibility that Americans would also be having veterans of our own post 9-n war in Afghanistan. I invited Dr. Rahman to join me for dinner at my River House during his visit to the University of Colorado. Out of respect for his Islamic beliefs, I offered no alcohol, and porcine products were nowhere on our menu.

Dr. Rahman had written several articles on subjects relating to peace and reconstruction in Afghanistan and was interested to hear of my work with Russian veterans of war in his country. This tall, elegant westernized gentleman, with carefully trimmed beard and mustache, was educated at Oxford University in the UK. I was delighted to learn that his favorite places in England were along those long stretches of Cornish coast where I have deep ancestral roots. My guest described his ethnic affiliation as belonging to a Pashtun tribe residing in the region nearest Pakistan. Pashtun represent the largest of Afghan ethnic groups and have traditionally produced most of their country's leaders.

At that time, Dr. Rahman was father to fifty children, having adopted all of his nieces and nephews after all of his brothers were killed during the Russian invasion. During this subsequent period of occupation, he explained that an entire generation had been "lost." Afghan social structure was totally shattered, schooling non-existent, and family and village life so damaged and disrupted that he deeply feared a return to Islamic fundamentalism as a hysterically controlled response to an all-pervasive chaos.

Dr. Rahman's fears were well founded, as the following decade would reveal when a Taliban regime seized control of his country. He foresaw no end to strife in his homeland anywhere in the foreseeable future. Part of this complex problem, he explained, was geographical. Afghanistan is located astride land routes between the Indian sub- continent, Iran and Central Asia. This region, repeatedly criss-crossed by armies, empire builders and trades routes has attracted conquerors throughout history. Modern day Mghanistan maintains a strategic importance due, in part, to the fact that it borders Iran, Turkenistan, Uzbekistan, Tajikistan, Pakistan and China. Over the years, I have often wondered if and how this good man survived subsequent and inevitably ongoing upheavals.

Tuning Board

Knowing that a second Russian invitation was imminent, Darrell and I had spent several busy months evolving our Relative Balance work. In turn, the process itself slowly began moving us in several new directions. We continued to work with our premise that trauma, in leaving its impact throughout a physical body, may therefore visibly manifest in various forms of imbalance, asymmetry, compression or torsion. We had discovered that creative movement work with various forms of distortion and imbalance can be an important step toward regaining lost postural and defensive reflexes that can occur during any process of overwhelm. Building upon our experiences with Swiss Balls, Darrell devised another kinesthetic tool.

Darrell reasoned that our adult human structure and nervous system is designed to orient in an upright posture. While Swiss physio-balls are excellent for sitting or lying, one cannot safely stand on them and reproduce the same sensations of buoyancy with both subtlety and safety. With this new device, one can stand. Darrell's original design consisted of two pieces of plywood glued on either side of a four-inch thick "sandwich" layer of foam rubber. This foam was of such a density that when a person of average weight stands on top of the board, the underlying foam gives, and this sets up a gentle rocking motion. The top surface of this board was lined with a simple "British Flag" design. This floor design is used in dance and creative movement to assist the performer's orientation in space (see www.acst-europe.com).

This orienting design indicates eight basic directions radiating from a center. A central circle represents our vertical center of gravity surrounded by a "core field". This pattern is intended to help people visualize an effortless, erect posture organized around a vertical axis through the center of their body. Extended vertically, the British Flag design can assist with a visualization of three cardinal planes of orientation, the sagittal, frontal and horizontal This can further disoriented and overwhelmed individuals to gradually re-orient to a three dimensional geometry of space while in a standing posture.

Since I had spent many hours on his "foam sandwich board", Darrell asked me to try to give a name to my experience. What immediately came to me was a sense of "attunement". This is important in the sense that attunement with nature, healthy orienting and defensive responses – a balanced deployment of instinctual responses to eat, mate, explore and defend, can be thrown out of balance when one is traumatized.

Attunement is critical for assuring appropriate and timely responses to both opportunity and danger. At the most basic level, it means survival. Darrell's deceptively simple device was designed as another means of assisting trauma survivors to find their way home to a felt sense of self through their perceptual responses native to a human organism. And so, from this experience of "attunement", Darrell's board became "The Tuning Board."

With Cliff at Mountain Air, I had discovered the value of introducing moderately difficult tasks, while out in the natural world, to gently bring trauma survivors into present time and explore their own particular resources for coping with physical limitations and discomforts as well as working through fears. Mindful attention to oneself and the task can provide a powerful catalyst for healing. Like the Swiss balls, Darrell's Tuning Board also presented a moderately difficult task, which could be used within a clinical setting.

One basic exercise is to ask a person to stand quietly and just look at the board. Their visual perception is usually of a round, solid and completely stable structure. They are then invited to step onto this board whenever they feel ready to do so. In this process of transferring weight onto the board, they suddenly realize that the surface that they are attempting to stand upon is in motion. This realization evokes a conscious perception that "things are not always what they seem." Now, our person must process information acquired directly from the feet, not through thought or visual perception. Originating in the feet, information must now travel through the entire length of the nervous system before arriving at the brain.

The organism will then become activated and immediately begin some sort of coping/orienting response in an attempt to orient and stabilize. Initially, an attempt to control the experience comes through extrinsic, cognitive and visual effort. An attempt is made to stabilize and control the board to make it stable and force it to match their original perception. In so doing, the person is trying to make the external world fit into their internal reality.

The Tuning Board, however, is designed to never be totally stable. There will always be some motion involved while standing on its surface. In assessing capability, it is important to observe how a person responds to that inevitability. They may find that some degree of extrinsic conscious control is possible. This level of mastery is particularly important when the board is used as a device to retrain neurostructural alignment patterns and response capabilities.

Mastery of this board, however, does not lie in its extrinsic control. If one remains with an extrinsic emphasis the board can quickly become boring. Real mastery resides in experiencing and trusting non-conscious, reflexive responses of a balanced standing posture with weight evenly distributed throughout both legs.

Returning to the initial experience, realization that a seemingly stable surface is in motion, and will stay that way, offers a cognitive challenge. This challenge lies in how an individual will accept and respond to this continuous motion. It is important to continue tracking until our person arrives at a point of relative stability. This can happen in a relatively short time. The idea is to encourage a basic skill of managing relative stability while standing on a moving board. This also presents a decision point for the tracker. Does our person have sufficient resources to explore a more challenging experience of motion and response?

If so, our next step is to ask our person to close their eyes while remaining on the board. At this point, much more movement, usually a swaying, occurs and there is a shift into a more internally oriented response to whatever disorientation results from lack of visual reference. This sets in motion another cycle of arousal and orientation. This next level of challenge moves away from cognitive toward the somatic while entering a realm of reflexes and responses. The tracker may need to move closer in order to ensure safety, as swaying may become significant with eyes closed. Continue on, is our new protocol, until relative stability is reached with eyes closed.

This brings a tracker to another decision point. At this stage it is important to assess an individual's resources in *exploring* the realm of response without use of visual references. This kind of work with the board, then, is done, in two major stages. The first is working within a realm of extrinsic, visual, cognitive experience. The second involves work with a more intrinsic, somatic experience. Second stage has much more movement associations with it.

On another level, this second stage can be seen as a challenge of moving from an orientation which seeks absolute stability and control, toward a "crisis of surrender" with a felt experience of encountering a reality of partial control and relative stability. This new way of being would include a felt sense of becoming structural and fluid, as well as boundaried and open.

It is during this intrinsic second stage that a wave-like motion will begin to appear throughout a standing posture. This motion starts in a person's feet, travels up through both legs, through the spinal cord and into the brain as a somatic experience, in contrast to solely cognitive action. This intrinsic wave-like motion cannot happen in an extrinsic, cognitive mode. In a Taoist sense, the organism is invited to move "out of fixation, into flow."

And so, a wave-like motion provides an integrated, resilient and intrinsic response experience in neural sensory motor associations, in the form of a new *engram* for relative balance. The role of engrams provides ongoing challenges in the understanding of the somatic manifestations of trauma. An engram may be defined as a definite or permanent trace left by a stimulus in the protoplasmic nerve tissue. Engrams, are in some functional and anatomical respects, at the opposite end of the behavioral spectrum from the primitive orienting reflexes which carry patterns established over millions of years of species development, and are re-created during the unfolding of every normal fetus (Juhan 1987; see also Schacter 1982).

Engrams are largely created from the life experience of every individual. In this sense, the term engram was used by Karl Lashley to describe the physical basis of long-term memory. Unlike orienting reflexes, engrams cannot be localized into any anatomical unit or fixed connection. Engrams are a means of arranging into meaningful sequences the firings of the more primitive reflexes. Engrams, therefore, are organizing factors that cannot be pinpointed. In many ways they are analogous to quarks in the realm of particle physics - "the ghosts in the machine" the direct observation of which has so far eluded us, but whose practical effects are everywhere evident (ibid.; see also Bartenieff Lewis 1980).

So, with the Tuning Board experience, the developing engram for relative balance addresses a geophysical truth that earth offers only relative stability. Upon stepping off the board onto "solid ground" one question is, "What has changed?" What role is cognition now playing in a standing posture? Now, there is more somatic information available. When on solid ground, an experience of relativity remains. This experience, which was not there before the board, can become a new reflexive response. Knowing in a felt sense that the Earth is only relatively stable, and moving, while feeling the planet move, as we move, is movement with a felt sense of relatedness and relationship.

In working with a Tuning Board, the human organism can learn to orient within a reality that things are not always as they appear. Attempts to orient toward a balanced, stable predictable reality, using only cognitive and visual perceptions, can lead to ongoing disorientation. In dealing with potentially traumatic situations, which are inherently unstable, unpredictable and often not as they initially appear, those organisms able to orient within a felt sense of relativity are much better prepared to respond. In a sense, an engram for Relative Balance, achieved through an intrinsically felt sense, can potentially serve as something like a "booster vaccine" which enhances immune responses by increasing capability.

The Tuning Board can be very valuable in training people to stay calm and centered with attention to their orienting reflexes under circumstances perceived as threatening. By learning to cultivate a deep intrinsic sense of balance, one can develop an expanded sense of option whenever the flight or fight reflex is activated. In this sense, a Tuning Board serves as a transitional object designed to access a subtle response to the geophysical forces of our gravitational field while in a standing posture. This sense soon becomes available without use of the board. We felt that Darrell's Tuning Board had the potential to expand options for non-verbal, kinesthetic, cross-cultural trauma work, and so he was willing to make ten of them for me to take along to Russia.

Sometime in early spring a message arrived from Valery. "Please come," his message said. "There is war in the Caucasus and much work to do." My mother was unhappy with this development. Over tea, she was predictably direct: "Who or what are you looking for in Russia? Our Cornish family has no Russian roots, and we have no family ties there." I said only what I understood to be my truth, "I don't really know." "The women in our family," she continued, "have always been involved in war. Did you know that three of your great aunts were nurses with the British Army in France during World War I?" I did not know that. What I did know was that they lived together, never married, and were considered to be somewhat "eccentric". And there was that scandalous business of their learning to smoke cigarettes.

No one, it seemed, had connected those few dots, which just may have indicated that these ladies' "eccentricities", might, just possibly, have had something to do with those unspeakable horrors of serving in a World War I field hospital. No morphine, emergency surgery without anesthesia, no antibiotics, a pervasive stench of gangrene and yes, I can imagine that they learned to smoke cigarettes. So many young men lost, in such a nightmare of horrifying conditions. And yes, I can imagine that as young women, my great aunts learned to shy away from attachment.

"So," my mother asked, "you are determined to return to Russia?" I told her that I was planning to return as soon as the passport and visa processes were complete. "Well then," she said, with painful reluctance, "I suppose that there is something you should know." I braced myself quietly, knowing that what was coming next would most likely be something, at the very least, unexpected.

Cornish people are secretive, because they had to be. Their conflict-ridden history with the English, combined with piracy, smuggling and many other factors, dating back to territorial intrigues during times of King Arthur, have mandated an insular culture of secrecy. If a Cornish person offers to disclose a secret, there must be a very important reason. If this Cornish person is your own mother, there can be no doubt that a major revelation is forthcoming. I held my breath and waited. "There were so many unknown factors surrounding your father's death," she explained, "I never really accepted those official reports. In my mind, he was always, in my imagination, somewhere or other in some Russian hospital." Her painful revelation needed to undergo many levels of integration before I was able to arrive at any degree of resolution for my mother and for myself.

In response to Valery's invitation and news of war in the

Caucasus between Georgia and Abkazia, I began my research into the history and culture of that region. The Eastern shores of the Black Sea are believed to be the location of the ancient Land of Colchis. According to an epic poem by Apollonius of Rhodes, 3rd century B. C., possibly derived from an earlier work by Pindar, it was here that Jason and the Argonauts sailed from Greece through the Dardenelle Straits in search of a Golden Fleece. Jason was sent on this suicide mission by a jealous uncle. Jason's given task was to capture a Golden Fleece whose magi- cal powers offered healing, protection and power to its possessor. This fleece was to be found hanging from a tree in a sacred grove, guarded by a :fire-breathing dragon who never slept. A similar legend also appears in Euripides's tragic drama, *Medea* (Severin 1986).

It seems that some form of a Golden Fleece may have actually existed. Local natives had a long tradition of using sheepskins to capture grains of alluvial gold flowing in their rivers. These fleeces were then dried and beaten in order to release their precious particles. In both ancient and modem times this area is known for excellence in metallurgy. This story continues as the Argonaut enlists aid from a daughter of the Colchian king, a princess and sorceress named Medea who fell in love with Jason and, in some versions, he with her. Tragedy results, as Medea kills her brother, betrays her family, puts the dragon to sleep with volatile vapors of a magic potion, and then flees with her lover and their stolen fleece (Koromila 1992).

An agenda such as this does not bode well for any relationship and, over time, Jason was to betray Medea with another woman. In revenge, Medea murdered their two children, and then, through sorcery, murdered Jason's newly betrothed. Again, as with Adam and Lilith, we have the fearful vengeance of an excluded and disrespected previous partner, and this time, the disastrous consequences for children are clear, on any kind of actual or metaphorical level. In search of power, Jason seized the coveted fleece through treachery, betrayal and deceit. Beyond this transient victory, we find yet another tragic episode in history's long tradition of men, women and war, and the war between men and women.

I felt that it was important to understand stories of a Golden Fleece, so integral to the culture in this Caucasian region, where ethnic war was currently raging. I also sensed that there was something in this legend of a Golden Fleece that offered insights into the complex realms of power struggle and gender. Dreaming this myth along, I then turned to another; a much more feminine version, with a very different outcome. In the myth of Eros and Psyche, there has been a breach of trust between married lovers. A desperate Psyche seeks aid from a reluctant Aphrodite, her husband's mother, in working toward a path of reconciliation. The Goddess of Love then assigns a series of seemingly impossible tasks. Here, we find an entirely different understanding of the lessons and power of the Golden Fleece.

One of many healing tasks is that Psyche must gather golden wool from the Sun Rams, who are notoriously fierce in the light of the mid-day sun. These aggressive Sun Rams represent what the Chinese might call yang; that rational, and aggressive, manifesting power of the masculine. In despair, Psyche sits down beside a riverbank in order to lament her fate. After a while, gentle flowing river reeds softly begin whispering their message.

"Sun Rams are fierce in the light of a noonday sun. Wait, patiently until the heat of the day has cooled and music of our river has lulled them into gentle receptivity. Then, and only then, may you safely cross the river, walk amongst them, and gather their precious golden wool from thorn bushes through which they have passed during their day."

Patiently, Psyche does wait, until a cooler yin part of the day begins with a slow setting of the sun. Only then, does she dare to cross this flowing divide, and gather her golden treasure, which she humbly presents to Aphrodite. While Psyche's struggles are far from over, she has learned an important lesson in her need for respect and timing in order to achieve a satisfactory interaction between the vastly different energies of masculine and feminine (Scott 1991). This lesson was to prove invaluable for me, as well, during my upcoming return to Russia.

Initially, my second transition, was considerably less difficult than my first. Again, Valery appeared together with Nellia to greet me at Moscow Airport. Pale with exhaustion, his sleepy melancholy eyes were now swollen with dark circles close to the color of old bruises. My first impression was of someone looking much like a bleary boxer who had been in the ring for too many rounds. At home, his wife and their children were hurt and angered by his frequent absences and war-weary exhaustion. Their domestic atmosphere was smogged with reproach and long periods of melancholy silence. When the time felt right, I asked about civil war in the former Soviet Republics and in the Caucasus.

The Caucasus region, Valery explained, has been an international focus for a number of projects involving oil and gas pipelines, railroads, airports, and communications networks that stretch all the way from Central Europe to China. Overall, the Caucasus represents a corridor crucial to the economic stability of Eurasia. There are at least five sides, he explained, who have something at stake in this region; Islamic terrorists hiding out in Chechnyna, Russia, Georgia, Abkazia, and your own USA.

More specifically, Valery went on, this primarily Christian region, now known as Abkazia was forcibly joined to Georgia by Stalin in 1931. The Abkazian coast became a favorite holiday retreat for Russian premiers, their loved ones and other higher-ups within the Soviet echelon. Stalin had Georgian roots as did Laverenty Beria, his head of Soviet Secret Police, who oversaw a policy of ethnic cleansing. When Khruschev came into power he reversed all of these anti-Abkazian policies.

Following the collapse of the former USSR, Abkazia was denied autonomy. Named for the Abkhaz peoples, native to this region, the local population reserved their right to differentiate themselves from Georgians and continue to pursue their own culture and to speak their own language. In 1992 Abkazia attempted an armed secession and the Georgians were unable to prevent them from going. This secession was achieved at a great price, amidst violence and a massive exodus of refugees.

On a household level there were many mixed marriages between Abkazians and their Georgian and Russian neighbors. At the village level, however, there remained a strong tendency toward ethnically compact populations. This patchwork population and scattered pat- terns of fighting gave rise to a war that was highly localized and intensely personal. For Abkazians, their struggle was marked by intolerance, revenge and fear of ethno-cultural genocide (Kolga 2002).

"We have civil war in our former republics, our clinic has no money, and many staff members are gone," Valery explained, "so I offer you a promotion. Together with me, you will be our co-director for a Civil War

Trauma Recovery project." In America, promotions are very important and carry increases in prestige, salary and power. In Russia, I knew by now, my promotion meant that I was no longer a guest. Like other doctors, without salary, I would cook and clean.

Over tea with Valery, I shared my mother's revelations of ongoing fears that my father, who would then have been in his late seventies, was to be found in some Russian hospital. (Mercifully, she never imagined him in a gulag, as was the fate of all too many prisoners of war.) Valery's immediate and unexpected response sailed me right over an edge into some version of a Russian "Twilight Zone". "Your Mother is right", he proclaimed, without hesitation. "War wounded Vanya" (Russian spelling of my father's name Vayne) "is in a Russian hospital and I will take you to him."

Somewhere between shock and gratitude, I accepted his offer. On our way to a huge government hospital in Moscow, with Nellia along for interpreting, Valery began to talk about his father "Iron Mike". His father, he explained, had been a patient in this hospital that we were about to visit. During the war with invading Germans, his father had stepped on a land mine that essentially shredded both of his legs. Upon news that he was missing in action, his mother, a medical doctor, had trekked over hundreds of miles to find her son. When she found him, near death, she carried him on her back to the relative safety of their nearest Russian field hospital.

After the war, Valery's father walked on artificial legs, miles to and then miles from medical school. Valery has vivid memories of his father's eagerness to rest after long walks and give his bruised and bloody stumps some recovery time. The irony, Valery relates, is that relief came only with the advent of German manufactured prostheses that fit so well that most of his father's daily pain was considerably lessened. This was especially important because Mikhail Semenovitch Mikhailovsky (1924-1995) was a surgeon who needed to spend many hours on his feet in an operating room. One needs to understand, with such a truly heroic father, "can't" was never an option for his offspring, and there was no such thing as an acceptable excuse.

As we arrived at a huge government hospital in Moscow Valery explained that the Abkazian ward was located in a remote wing of this monolithic structure. Just before we went in, I asked why the Abkazian soldiers were in an especially remote ward. Valery pretended that he did not hear my question. I had come to accept this selective hearing as the usual Russian response from anyone who did not want to answer questions. This had been an ongoing problem for me, as an American. We are information junkies, and Russians are most decidedly nothing of the sort. Like my Cornish relatives, Russian people are secretive, but for very different reasons. Cornish people know and don't tell. Russians don't want to know and therefore, can't tell. As a result, in need of a survival strategy, they have cultivated a culture of individual and collective denial.

Reluctantly, and with a considerable degree of embarrassment, Nellia, our interpreter explained that, in Russia, information is a problem. Even now, an ominous Stalinist/ KGB legacy remains "in the field", and no one wants any kind of information that could mean trouble for themselves, their families or their neighbors. People with information often just disappeared sometime during the middle of some night, along with their entire families. All official record of their existence also disappeared. My American pattern of asking many questions had been an ongoing source of tension. "Do you remember," Nellia asked, "that episode where there was a coup and Mr. Gorbachev disappeared for a while"? I did, indeed. "Well," she continued, "on Russian television, for over a week, our news reports were replaced with 24-hour re-runs of the Swan Lake ballet. You need to understand that any request here for sensitive information is likely to be met with 'swan feathers'." For Russians," she said very quietly, "people from the Caucasus are considered to be black, and we don't really want them here."

Duly informed, I followed Valery through long cavernous corridors of this Kafka-esque, huge monstrosity of a hospital until we arrived at the Abkazian ward. These patients were all male and had sustained serious injuries including loss of limbs from stepping on land mines and were waiting to be fitted for prosthetic devices. Our arrival was a non- event. The air in this ward was thick with tobacco smoke and muffled sounds from a small black-and-white TV blaring on about something to do with sports. It was immediately clear that these Abkazian patients were seriously drunk on whatever vodka they had managed to obtain. No one bothered to look in our direction as we slowly found chairs and quietly took seats facing several rows of hospital beds. "Vanya!" Valery exclaimed in a rush of recognition. Off in a distant comer, he recognized an older man, probably somewhere in his late seventies. He had olive skin, clear green eyes and a magnificent head of thick wavy hair. I went into some state of shock. This Vanya, so resembled my father Vayne, who might have looked much like this at this age, had he lived. Here, unmistakably incarnate, was my mother's fantasy of my father lying wounded in a Russian hospital.

Vanya, just hours before, had surgery on his stumps which had begun to "pencil". Sometimes in the case of traumatic amputations, bones begin to poke and point their way through remaining layers of skin. At this time, there were no anesthetics or painkillers available, not even aspirin. Vanya' s only choice was to make do with vodka, throughout his painful ordeal. Now, he sat up in bed, absolutely straight. He embraced Valery and remembering a promise, given by Valery, in Abkazia, that with Russian help, Vanya would walk again. Vanya ignored the stream of tears that he could not control. "Listen," Vanya commanded these young soldiers, "there are people here who can help you. Turn off your TV, stop your drinking and smoking and listen to what they have to say." Because, Vanya was an elder in their culture, without question, these young men obeyed.

They all agreed to come to our clinic for treatment and also to participate in our nature programs located deep within the Russian forest. Vanya only wanted to go home. There is no doubt that without Vanya's fatherly and authoritative intervention, none of these young soldiers would have bothered to leave their TV, drug, alcohol and war-induced hospitalized trance in order to follow us to the forest. Vanya appeared, in this painful setting, as a wise elder. "I am only grateful," he maintained, "that I, as an old man, stepped on that mine that took my legs. Better me, than some young person with a long, active life still ahead."

Yes, and now I understood that both Valery and my mother were right. My "father" was in a Russian hospital. Vaynej Vanya had appeared as an archetype of a powerful father figure, at a crucial time where there was much elder guidance and healing needed for young people, in their ever-present realm of war trauma. Strange as it may seem, both my mother and I were able to draw deep solace from this very real and also surreal reality.

Upon our return to the Center, as requested, I gave

a Tuning Board lecture/demo during an early morning gathering of volunteer staff, professionals from the community and interested patients. Their response was, at best, indifferent. Had this been my first trip to this Russian clinic, I would have been very discouraged. By now, however, I had some sense of the protocol. Overall, it was agreed that my presentation was "useless and not Russian." Valery dismissed my offering as a mere "reinvention of Taoism." "This," he maintained, "offers nothing to our Abkazian and other soldiers who have lost lower limbs."

Like Psyche, I withdrew to my "riverbank" directly across the street from the clinic and waited for an atmospheric change. The "Sun Rams" were fierce indeed, in the light of morning sun. Silently, I withdrew in search of whatever rest and reflection I could find within the calm of my apartment space. Patiently, I waited for nightfall, which in Zelenograd, in summer, meant that their local sun would set sometime just before or after midnight.

After a quiet retreat from the clinic, I had a few hours of much needed "time out" and rest. Just before midnight, there was a loud knocking, and I answered my door. Vodka in hand, bottles of Russian champagne arrived along with Valery, Nellia, and Sergei and Anatoly. This gathering went into the wee hours and this was to be our pattern for the remainder of my visit. The real work of our Russian exchange happened sometime during those very *yin* hours between midnight and 4 AM. Out of necessity, I learned to adapt to this rhythm, leaving the clinic in late afternoon and resting for several hours before my visitors arrived.

These late-night visits were not part of Nellia's job description, and she came along because she "didn't want to miss anything." While the men were taking their smoking breaks outside on the balcony, Nellia and I had some private time to talk. Mostly, I listened. "Your ball work," she began, "which gently addresses the trauma to the pelvic diaphragm, is so important for Russian women." Nellia went on to explain that in Russia, there really is no reliable method of birth control. Pharmacological options are not available in form of birth control pills or spermicides.

"These are things that only some of us read about in the foreign press. Russian men refuse to use our rough, thick and decidedly unsenusal condoms, which really aren't easily available, anyway. We have no service that offers other barrier methods such as your western diaphragms. And so," she continued, "our dominant method for birth control is abortion."

"This is difficult," she explained, "because these procedures are performed without anesthetic and many sexually active Russian women have had between 1 0 and 15 of these abortions. The pain of this ruins relationships. Russian men complain that Russian women are "cold". "Who could really warm again to an intimate relationship that had been scarred with this kind of pain? Please understand," she asked, "that we have a long history of denial."

Nellia continued to describe her fears about the growing fear of SIDS, the Russian abbreviation for AIDS. She was afraid that the blood supply was contaminated and also needles used for vaccinations, mostly to children, were being re-used, and the HIV virus spread. Deeply moved by these conversations, I brought these concerns to Valery. Not surprisingly, he suddenly became both deaf and distracted. Russian face, again, along with an ample flurry of swan feathers.

I had an image of those three monkeys, "Hear No Evil, See No Evil and Speak No Evil" sitting in some archetypal troika firmly entrenched somewhere between the two of us.

And yes, I did know that a Russian sense of loyalty to Mother Russia extended to one's family as well, and one just did not speak of "family matters" outside this circle.

Dark Truths

We reach for the bright truth, and hardly pay attention that it actually limits, excludes, and dazzles us. The dark truth, with blurred borders, is more exact. It makes us be more awake, just as when we move around in the dark, we are prompted to be open to all of our senses.

Bert Hellinger

With no particular attention to the date, I arrived at the Center on the morning of June 22, 1993. An all-pervasive atmospheric pall was nearly overwhelming. Our normal bustle of morning activity was muted, and people were pale and moving slowly, as though in shock. Nellia had not yet arrived, and I asked Sergei to explain the situation. Although initially astonished that I could be unaware of the importance of this date, Sergei chose to arise above a cultural layer of polite consternation. With some mixture of English and Russian, he explained that this day was an anniversary of the "violation of Mother Russia": the German invasion of June 22, 1941.

Still, I was having difficulty understanding, why so many people, some of whom who were not even alive at that time, were having such strong reactions. The emotional fog and funereal mood was that of a very recent event. And yet, I was slowly learning that Russian people bond through suffering and tragic events, which are either collectively denied or collectively grieved. Valery arrived quite a bit later, a some- what absent presence, something like a ghost of himself. His distracted and disheveled appearance, faded into an impenetrable silence. It was clear that there would be no more work for us that day. I left early and retired to the relatively safe distance within my seemingly neutral, dun-colored apartment.

My emotional compass was spinning. Turning toward my literary resources, I realized that, for me, they are often most intriguing when they are able to transcend both linguistic and cultural borders. Feeling an urgent need to re-orient within my own American culture, I turned to the rough hewn voice of Edward Abbey, who lists Tolstoy and Solzhenitsyn amongst his literary heroes. Thumbing through *One Life at a Time, Please* (1978), I found some thoughts about "us and them":

"Easy enough to point out and condemn the faults and crimes of other nations The Soviet Union and the United States, while by no means morally equivalent, are basically similar in structure and purpose. Both societies are dedicated to nationalism, militarism, industrialism, technology, science, organized sport, and above all, the religion of growth- of endless expansion in numbers, wealth, power, time and space. In the SU, government controls industry; in the US, industry controls government; but each of the two superstates is ruled by an entrenched oligarchy- in the SU by the Communist Party, in the US by the power of concentrated wealth ...

Our century, the twentieth, has been a century of horrors. The century not only of Stalin's gulag but of Hitler's concentration camps, where six million Jews, three million Russians, two million Poles, and a half a million Gypsies were methodically put to death. But America has done its bit; last nation on earth to abolish chattel slavery (and it required a civil war to accomplish that), and we were the first to drop the nuclear bomb on our fellow humans, the Japanese, *after* their government had begun suing for peace ... Our slaughters do not yet equal in magnitude those of Stalin or Hitler – but we tried, and are trying, and we're not finished yet. Meanwhile the threat of nuclear annihilation, succeeded by the nuclear winter, hangs over the entire planet, with the devices of destruction continually being developed, refined, and stockpiled on both sides. On several sides."

Exhausted, I fell into an uneasy sleep. Late that evening, Valery arrived unannounced, with Nellia, and a warm bottle of Russian black market champagne. "Tonight," he announced, "we drink to some miracles of survival, and I will tell you a long dark story of history of this day for Russian, Ukrainian and Jewish people." Valery had not been sleeping well for the previous week and during daylight had experienced recur- ring visions of the German Luftwaffe looming overhead. He could "hear" the ominous drone of enemy aircraft and could do little to mute his overwhelming feelings of dread.

On June 22, 1941, Hitler's "Operation Barbarossa: Drive to The East" attacked the western borders of Belarus and Ukraine. This offensive carried along the Nazi contagion for eliminating all "sub-human species" such as Jews. In 1939 the Jewish population of Ukraine was 1.5 million, accounting for approximately 3% of their total citizenry.

At the outbreak of this terrible invasion, the Soviet government hastily arranged for a massive evacuation of key personnel, East, to Russia. These evacuees included approximately 2/3 of the Ukrainian Jewish population (Boshyk 1986).

At the very last minute, Valery's Jewish grandparents were able to secure passage for their son, on one of these evacuations. Valery's father, barely 17 years of age, obeyed his family, boarded a train, and eventually found his way to Dagestsan. Soon thereafter, Nazi *Einsatzgruppen* arrived in their region of The Ukraine. These specialized, mobile killing squads arrived with orders, in the service of The Final Solution, to kill all Jews. During that summer of 1941, many members of Valery's father's family perished along with more than 600,000 Ukrainian Jews.

Mikhail Simenovich Mikhailovsky arrived, alone, in the Dagestani capital of Makchachkula in a northeast section of the Caucasus Range, somewhere along the shores of the Caspian Sea. Dagestan has one of the oldest Jewish communities in the former USSR, tracing their history back to Persia, with their ancestors having lived in this region since the 5th Century A. D. (Kolga 2002). Young Mikhailovsky was soon drafted into a Russian army vigorously engaged in a desperate struggle to expel all German invaders. This, I now understood, was the first part of his family history that Valery had shared at the military hospital and how it was that his father had come to encounter a land mine that destroyed his legs while fighting in the Caucasus. Along with war, there was also the overwhelming tragedy of genocide. For Valery, these painful memories of personal and cultural history mandated a cross-cultural approach to trauma with assistance available to those in need, irrespective of ethnic or religious affiliation.

Tensions were high and tempers short at The International Center School of Rehabilitation just before the arrival of our Abkazian guests. We were expecting soldiers who had encountered land mines, along with several members of Abkazia's embassy in Moscow. Volunteers and a few remaining staff at the Center were resisting our War Trauma Recovery Project. Their first line of objection was that these Abkazians were not "real soldiers", only partisans in a civil conflict that had nothing to do with Mother Russia. Valery countered by reminding everyone present that this trauma center was international and cross-cultural. "We are in the business of healing," he reiterated and "only healing. We are not politicians, nor are we judges. Our business is only with the wounded and their loved ones."

Somewhat sheepishly, Nellia told me, during a quiet moment, that the real issue was racial discrimination. No one wanted to welcome or work with these "blacks". She herself would never agree to this project, except for her interest in trauma work. "Nice Russian girls," she offered, "are warned against these Caucasian predators who only want to marry us in order to obtain permits to live in Russia."

Valery was clear. The project would go forward. Anyone unwilling to abide by the stated objectives of his clinic was welcome to leave, immediately. No one left, although an unspoken drizzle of resentment permeated the atmosphere. And then, quite unexpectedly, Anatoly appeared with a generous basket of fresh eggs. He did not speak, nor did he need to. This mountainous, rough-hewn, authoritative, decidedly shamanic presence carried a non-negotiable message of support that no one dared challenge.

In time, our Caucasian guests arrived. Along with their traumatized amputees, the Abkazian Embassy in Moscow had sent two interpreters, Liana and Arda. Translation was essential to our project since we were navigating at least three languages, Russian, English and Abkazian. Liana had been a professor of English literature at the University before Georgians closed it down. Arda also spoke English and was one of five psychologists in their fledgling Republic of Abkazia. This entourage was overseen by the somewhat bulky and ever shadowy figure of Rassoul, whose duties were to remain unspecified. It was somehow understood that he was an important conduit for transmission of both medicine and arms from Russia to their Abkazian front.

From this alliance, I was to discover the value of cross-cultural work that included at least three cultures. Had we been working only with a Russian-American coalition we could have easily fallen into polarization and subsequent power struggles. With three cultures and three languages involved, we were always grounded in an absolute necessity of remaining extremely spacious and always flexible.

The Abkazians arrived in Red Cross vehicles, and we all went out to welcome them and their drivers. In Russia, protocol demands inclusion. Their Russian drivers, however, opted for a "time out" and withdrew. These Abkazian, so-called, "black" people, I noticed, although mostly dark haired, with even darker eyes, had very pale skin, several shades lighter than my own olive complexion. As a group, Nellia shared, she found them to be remarkably handsome, indeed. In spite of her culturally induced reservations, she could only admire their slender frames, fine bones and delicate features. This realization left her understandably embarrassed and confused.

It was agreed that the Abkazian soldiers would reside at the clinic for the duration of our project. It was soon clear that they expected to continue their "hospital lives" in the same manner as in the military unit in Moscow. They slept little and spent most of night drinking vodka and smoking hashish. When I arrived in the morning they were barely awake in no mood for anything new. Valery had been up most of the night, as well, and dismissed my objections to drugs and alcohol. "For now," he said, "we have to allow them to self-medicate. These men are in pain, and we cannot begin by denying them the only relief they know." He sharply reminded me that here in Russia there are no pain medicines, not even aspirin, nor anti-depressants or any other kind of psychotropic drugs. "And," he continued, "just what exactly do you have to offer these men that could compete with these familiar pain relievers?"

This, of course, was an important question. Being a woman and a foreigner whatever credibility I had with these Abkazian men was granted only through my affiliation with a Russian male doctor. Their distinctly macho culture did not permit any open acknowledgment of pain and suffering, and to admit to being traumatized was tantamount to admitting that one was weak, insane and shamefully out of control. Psychological work was not acceptable and there were also obvious limitations of language.

Valery softened when he saw that I wasn't going to argue. I with- drew from any atmosphere of confrontation and just set up a number of Tuning Boards and physio-balls and then just sat by our samovar for a quiet cup of smoky Russian caravan tea. Gradually, over the course of our morning, the Abkazians discovered both balls and boards and spontaneously began to experiment with balance. Like our previous group of women without legs that I had worked with during my last visit, these men were intuitively drawn to these challenges and opportunities inherent within an experience of relative balance.

Valery joined me in a quiet place of non-intrusive observation. "These people", he said, "come from high mountains and their sense of balance has been bequeathed through many generations. In rediscovering their own sense of center, they also discover a deep sense of "home" which has a connection to the felt sense of earth, not specific to any time and place. Wholeness and home have a lot to do with healing after the shattering experiences of war. In this respect," he added, "nature often offers the best medicine."

The following day we joined Anatoly in his deep forest setting. Initially, the Abkazians were uncomfortable and unsure as to what they were supposed to do there. Anatoly quickly took charge and announced that he was especially pleased to welcome so many visitors because there was so much work to be done. He quickly assigned tasks of food preparation, setting up and stoking the samovar, building a fire under that huge iron caldron that hung above a wooden hearth. I immediately set forth into a nearby field to gather bouquets of wild flowers for Anatoly's hand-hewn long, strong, lovingly carved wooden tables.

Here again was this Russian model from which I learned so much. There was no obvious agenda, no visible technique or protocol and nothing in the way of a medical, psychological or psychiatric treatment plan. There would be no intake forms, no clinical assessments and no double blind or follow-up studies. These Russians understood that "broken connections" worked with the power and wisdom of a knowing and interactive field. Nature, community, good food, deep conversation and music created their container. In Russia there was always time for folk music and in this instance, for many songs of war and peace.

Over time, I was observing the awesome process of these combatants coming back into connection with themselves, with each other and others and the natural and social world surrounding them.

Nevertheless, I had my own biases and incessant thoughts about the obscenity of war as an ongoing struggle within myself. Intolerably restless, I followed Anatoly down to the lake to help with the rinsing of his huge baskets of rice. "Work hard," he roared, and "focus!" Every one of these grains of rice must be "very, very clean." Seeing that I was on the edge of overwhelm, this wise shaman insisted that I quiet my mind and bring awareness into present time. There was no need to explain my upset since I knew that he knew this issue all too well.

It was painful enough seeing these wounded young men, missing limbs and trying to find their way back to some sort of balance. My experiences with war trauma up until then had been only with the aftermath of war. And, these young men, I knew, were going back into combat. In this civil war, everyone was expected to participate, old and young, and women and wounded. In desperation, even prisons were emptied and inmates released into a field of battle.

"These men do not want or need your tears," Anatoly thundered, "you do them a disservice" and then, louder still "this isn't your war!" A clear intention was kindling in those dark eyes, and next came his announcement that if I did not pull myself together, and fast, I was going to be thrown into the lake. This "intervention" made it much easier to focus on very, very clean rice.

Coming to any sort of peace on the subject of war was a process that unfolded over decades. It all came together for me in Germany many years later in Wurzburg when I heard Bert Hellinger address the subject of "War and Peace" (4th International Conference on Systemic Constellations, 2003): "All wars are the wars of the gods. And these gods have many names. Democracy, Communism, National Socialism, Christianity, Judaism, Islam and so forth ... And all of these gods demand sacrifice ..."

I returned to our hearth with several baskets of

nearly immaculate rice which was to form the base of a huge vegetarian dish that Anatoly would patiently simmer in his immense black iron cauldron. Valery and the Abkazian soldiers were euphoric after a successful round of diving and swimming in the lake. Somehow, these men had an idea that their loss of limbs would mean that they would no long be able to swim and they were overjoyed to discover that this was not the case. Valery was pleased and appeared very relaxed and at home with their situation. After their time with us, these men would return to the military hospital in Moscow to have their final fittings for new prosthetic devices, and then return home, to their war.

In observing Valery's work with war-traumatized people, I often thought of Cliff and the ways that both seemed most alive when working with other people's pain. Over time, I came to realize that Valery and Cliff and many of my other colleagues who specialize in international trauma work often felt most alive in the midst of war, natural or man-made disasters or some other field of crisis. Gradually, I understood the seductive powers of intensity and crisis. In such situations there is no time to dwell upon one's own personal pain. In some ways crisis also serves as a kind of emotional undertow and pressure equalizer, where outside pain serves to offset and balance whatever pain may rest inside. There is something comforting about being in the presence of a pain that is greater than one's own.

This process, however, can become cumulative whereby the pain of others continues to be compounded with one's own, and so there is an ever-increasing need to find larger fields of intensity and crisis.

Eventually, one can find oneself only comfortable in the company of greater and greater pain. This pattern can prove disastrous for intimate partnerships and pragmatic routines of ordinary family life, and eventually many trauma specialists may become isolated from their loved ones. Over time, these patterns of ongoing intensity, overwork and isolation can lead to serious health problems, as bodies begin to break down. Emotional breakdown is a danger as well, which may manifest in a form of "Bum Out" and "Compassion Fatigue" where one just cannot bring oneself to care about anyone or anything anymore. The feeling is something like that of a boxer who has been in the ring for too many rounds and finds himself exhausted and "on the ropes". It is not surprising therefore that the most serious issue in the field of traumatology is how to keep people in the profession.

I kept these thoughts to myself while I was in Russia. It was clear that Valery saw his war trauma work as a mission and was more than willing to sacrifice marriage, family and friendship to this cause. Valery was to make two more trips to Abkazia that year to a field hospital near the front and then, on to Chechnya. Health care workers and surgeons there were totally overwhelmed, without adequate supplies for treating those acutely wounded combatants and victims who flooded their facility on an ongoing daily basis.

During our many late-night conversations, with both of us exhausted from our clinic day, I seem to remember Valery saying, something like ..." perhaps this work demands that one must move onto some level far above and beyond the personal ... a kind of inward clarity." Yes, I thought, this may be true for us, and, should our families and other loved ones, also be expected to accept this version of reality? Will our work also grant them some sort of inward clarity? I had my doubts.

Soon thereafter Valery left for a further series of trips to the battle- grounds of Chechnya. We lost touch over the years and, for a while, there was only one long war-weary letter about the devastated city of Grozny. Valery was organizing efforts to bury the dead and had been unable to return home for the death of his father:

"... years have passed since we have seen each other ... It seems to me that the number of events which happened in this period of time will be more than enough for another lifetime. As for my father, ... he passed away on June 6th ... during the last months of his life I happened to be very close to him, but I didn't manage to see him ... In March and April I was in Grozny- it is only 200 kilometers away from Makhachkala, but I failed to visit my parents because I had to take people who suffered from this damned war in Chechnya to my Center in Moscow. Later, I could not leave from Moscow because I had people living at the Center and I was trying to find solutions on many problems related to their stay. ... A certain process of accumulation has been going on within my inner self. It is high time to evaluate things happening all around. Though from the logical point of view many of the things going on in Russia nowadays are difficult to comprehend. Breakdown of the empire grew to geo-political boundaries.

Degradation literally penetrates all social groups and the society where redistribution of values is going according to uncertain laws. It could be possible to adjust to the unjust redistribution of material values for a great majority of people. But the most terrible thing is this disintegration in the spiritual sphere. Now all relations between people are based on materialistic issues, the general level of culture and science drops down, crimes grow.

Thank God, we now have a fragile peace in Chechnya. Lately, I visited the Northern Caucasus several times ... Probably, you have seen documentaries about Grozny nowadays and what it has turned into. At the entrance of the city one can see words written in huge letters on a concrete wall: 'Welcome to Hell'. This is true. This is Hell, indeed. This city has turned into a huge graveyard. People were buried in shell holes. One can see graves and corpses that still need to be buried. I had to participate in these burials, as well. Victims are numbered in hundreds of thousands. People were buried in common graves, too. Those graves were trenches several meters long. Hundreds of corpses were just put into them. Just seeing crowds of black crows flying above the graves and by breathing the stench of several hundred decomposing bodies in order to start hating war as the most disgusting thing going on during our lifetime.

It is a shame, but the reaction of most Russians is as if this is going on in another galaxy .... In Russia, they prefer to show American horror movies on TV.

Right now, I am in Moscow ... Experience that I got in Chechnya gave me a lot of information for meditation. Unfortunately, I have many more questions than answers. It is very exciting to work in the field of trauma. The deeper that I plunge into the theory of trauma, the most interested I feel. My own life challenges turned out to be definitive experiences, necessary for overcoming trauma. Translated by Bolonitkov, September 21, 1995 (50th anniversary of my father's death).

Such a letter! And those terrible crows gathering, yet, again! Now, however, I had come to understand something far beyond that dark gathering of scavenger birds just outside of my window during my terrified first arrival in Russia. Perhaps, now, I can begin to accept that it is true that souls grows through suffering and that these dark messengers are always somewhere, "in the contract."

Six years after our Abkazian war recovery project, Arda, a psychologist who had served as one of our interpreters was able to come to the US for more training in Tuning Board techniques. She brought news that all of "our" soldiers were alive and well. They had managed to establish a war recovery center of their own in the mountains of Abkazia using nature and community in the treatment of combat trauma. The political situation in Abkazia remained unsettled and Arda held no hope for change in any foreseeable future. While I was to return to Russia several times over the next decade, my Abkazian experience had proved pivotal in term of what was to follow. This was an important step in understanding which wars had something to do with me and those which I needed to leave to others. It had become increasingly clear that my work was really about myself, my family and an ongoing process of discovering what it means to be an engaged human being at this point in space and time.

Rilke, I knew, had understood this:

"Why? Because being here amounts to so much ... because all of this here and now so fleeting, seems to require us and strangely concerns us, the most fleeting of all ..."

(The Ninth Elegy)

My return to Colorado coincided with Peter Levine's return from his travels and we set aside some time to "touch base." He suggested some "camping" which, for us, meant building a small fire out along the North St. Vrain River, more like a creek during the summer months, that flowed along a gentle curve between his place and mine. "What's next?" he asked, and I replied that I had been invited to Germany. "Yes," he said, "the deepest healing for you may be there." And, yes, it was, and that is yet, another story.

Conclusion

"In a dark time, the eye begins to see ..."
Theodore Roethke

Throughout the evolution of my experiences with trauma, it has be- come increasingly clear that Nature offers those in the healing and helping professions a valuable, cross-culturally available resource for the understanding and healing of trauma. Nature offers all forms of healers and their clients many lessons in devastation and renewal. Most recently the seaquake/tsunami of December 26th 2004 presented the global challenge of coming to terms with a natural disaster powerful enough to alter the map of Asia, permanently accelerate planetary rotation, rattle our Earth's orbit and add an inch of tilt to an already wobbling axis. This tsunami represents both a major social and global trauma where effects extend far beyond individuals into their families, community, entire nations and the biosphere itself.

Beyond the devastation, our natural world also offers a wealth of healing resources. One can read the life history of a tree for example, according to the pattern of its rings, or find a map in the shell of an oyster, which tells the story of its life and relationship to the sea. I have come to believe that we are all rather like tree rings and shell patterns in that what has happened to us leaves a permanent record. The goal of trauma work, therefore, as I see it, is not to erase or cure but rather to expand to include and grow larger than whatever has happened to us. If one thinks in terms of integration and of resolving rather than eliminating trauma, then there is a possibility of guiding a multidimensional human organism, toward an experience of relative balance and resiliency.

For specialists willing to venture beyond the conventional container of official agency or private practice, the field of traumatology offers much in the way of opportunities and challenges to expand our understanding of the human condition. The process of translating my Relative Balance work in the natural world into methods involving both Tuning Board and Physio-balls was an important transition into a realm of cross-cultural, kinesthetic, non-verbal approaches to trauma. This I believe, is a necessary direction for those of us willing to address the needs of overwhelmed populations for whom individual psychotherapy is neither available, nor appropriate. Whatever the container, those brave souls willing to approach the enormous and ongoing challenge of individual and social trauma, would do well to heed the advice of my Chinese doctor Lam Kong. Dr. Kong is also a great Taoist Master, well versed in ancient wisdom and in the relative balance of female and male principles of Yin and Yang. "Most important," he cautions, "do not do more of what does not work." Clear and simple, the message is that "one size fits all" trauma recovery programs are not the answer. People have culturally specific as well as individual responses to overwhelming life events.

It is important for well intentioned professionals to bear in mind that with individual and social trauma work, it is essential to under- stand that "less is more", a quality which the Chinese may define as Yin. This quality appears in my earlier story of a rainmaker, who needed only enough receptivity, in order to "allow" the much-needed rain to fall. With any kind of approach to trauma, we must remember that it is essential to not do *anything* that may overwhelm an already overwhelmed individual, family, community or other social system. Our primary task is to assess for existing and potential resources and then find ways to restore some sense of relative balance. Over time, I have come to understand that encouraging or even insisting that over- whelmed people re-live their experiences and talk about their feelings is counterproductive and this approach often contributes to destructive cycles of re-traumatization.

The field of traumatology has been riddled from the outset with a wealth of "good ideas that just don't work." For this reason, it is important not to lead any therapeutic intervention with an emphasis on formula or technique. From my perspective, an essential goal of trauma work is to gradually find our way toward a meaningful integration of whatever has happened to us. This process is not about fixing people. Suffering human beings are not machines. Trauma is not something that we can expect our clients to "get over." In time, overwhelming experiences can become positively integral to who they are and to who they will become.

Clinicians need to continue to find ways to expand and include traumatic experiences from which one can draw strength and mean- ing. Healing and helping professionals and their clients have an opportunity to gain a particular kind of wisdom that I call "terrible knowledge." The only way to gain terrible knowledge is terrible and not something that most would consciously choose. Nevertheless, trauma survivors, and their caregivers who have this kind of wisdom, can become valuable teachers in the lessons of life. We live on a difficult planet, during challenging times, and it is just not possible to vaccinate or "trauma-proof" people against all of the kinds of overwhelm that can lead to trauma.

For those who want to engage in any kind of trauma therapy, it is important to understand that it is the quality of the contact that pre- pares the field for further work. A simple guideline for those wanting to provide assistance to the traumatized may be found in the wisdom of Mira Rothenberg, author of *Children with the Emerald Eyes.* Years ago, Mira offered a workshop focusing on work with traumatized children. One disgruntled participant complained, "But, Mira, you haven't given us any rules." "This is not about rules," she replied. "You show up, you shut up and you get what is going on. And, yes, it is best that you don't DO anything until you develop, at least, some grasp of what may be revealed as a very complicated situation." Simple, but not easy, for those whose primary orientation is toward action and problem solving. It is here that the voice of The Feminine, with an emphasis on attunement, receptivity, and a capacity to yield to the necessities of the moment, has much to offer.

For those of us who may find ourselves in the role of "outside experts", our situation requires a great sensitivity to the community and culture into which we are invited. My experience in Russia and other countries has been an ongoing lesson in the need to "join the culture" and align oneself with existing resources. One must take care not to send any sort of disempowering message that your host community does not have adequate resources to manage their overwhelm, or that you know better than they do what is best for them. Not only would this be a disrespectful, and potentially disempowering, stance, it would be counterproductive to the goal of fostering resources and resiliency.

In my work with trauma, I have come to accept that human misfortune and extreme experiences are part of

this reality of being alive. I feel that, all too often, these experiences lead to a diagnosis of Post traumatic Stress Disorder. Well-meaning individuals working with trauma need to understand that overwhelming experiences are not diseases in themselves. While it is true that these events can leave deep and potentially permanent scars, it is also true that people can recover and rebalance. Our capacity to rebound and transform traumatic experience is innate. How we meet such challenges can be an opportunity for both personal and societal transformation.

Bibliography

Achterberg, I. (1985): Imagery in Healing. Boston (New Science Library).
American Psychiatric Assocociation (1994): Diagnostic and Statistical Manual of Mental Disorders. Washington, D. C. (American Psychiatric Press),rev. 4th ed.
Angelou, M. (1993): On the Pulse of Morning. The Inaugural Poem. New York (Random House).
Arendt, H. (1973): On Revolution. Harmonsworth Middlesex (Penguin).
Ausbel, N. (1948): A Treasury of Jewish Folklore. New York (Crown).
Bartenieff I. with D. Lewis (1980): Body Movement: Coping With the Environment. New York (Gordon & Breach).
Boshyk, Y (Ed.) (1986): The Ukraine During World War II: History and its Aftermath. A Symposium (Canadian Institute of Ukranian Studies. University of Alberta).
Bykov, K. M. and W. H. Gantt (1957): The Cerebral Cortex and the Internal Organs. New York (Chemical Publishing).
"Can Russia Escape its Past". TIME Magazine Special Report (December 1992): 32-69.
Caputi, J. (1997): The Influence of Print Upon the European Witch Craze. Unpublished manuscript.
Carothers, A. (1991): "The Children of Chernobyl". Greenpeace Magazine (]anuary/ February): 8-13.
Charlesworth, J. R. (Ed.) (1983): The Old Testament Pseudepigrapha, Vol. I. Garden City, NY (Doubleday).
Christ, C. and J. Plaskow (1992): Womanspirit Rising: A Feminist Reader in Religion. San Francisco (Harper & Row).
Collier, A. L. (1885): Lilith: The Legend of the First Woman. Boston (Lothrop).
Colegrave, S. (1979): Uniting Heaven and Earth. A Jungian and Taoist Exploration of the Masculine and Feminine in Human Consciousness. Los Angeles (Tarcher).
Colodzin, B. (1989): Trauma and Survival: A Self Help Learning Guide. Laramie, WY (Ghost Rocks).
Cousins, N. (1981): Human Option. New York (Norton).
Dallett, J. O. (1988): When the Spirits Come Back. Toronto, Canada (Inner City).
Dallett, J. O. (1991): Saturday's Child: Encounters With Dark Gods. Toronto, Canada (Inner City)
Daly, M. (1978). Gyn-Ecology: The Metaethics of Radical Feminism. Boston (Beacon).

Danieli, Y. (1985): The Treatment and Prevention of Long Term Effects of Intergenerational Transmission of Victimization. A Lesson From Holocaust Survivors and Their Children. In: C. R.
Downing, C. (1981): The Goddess: Mythological Images of The Feminine. New York (Crossroad).
Ehrenreich, B. and D. English (1973): Witches, Midwives and Nurses.
Old Westbury, NY (Feminist Press).
Estes, C. P. (1992): Women Who Run With Wolves. Myths and Stories of the Wildwoman Achetype. New York (Ballantine).
Feitis, R. (Ed.) (1978): Ida Rolf Talks About Rolfing and Physical Reality. Boulder, CO (Rolf Institute).
Fesbach, M. and A. J. Friendly (1992): Ecocide in the USSR. Health and Nature Under Siege. New York (Basic Books).
Figley, C. R. (Ed.) (1985): Trauma and its Wake, Vol. I. New York (Brunner/Mazel).
Galland, C. (1990): Longing for Darkness: Tara and the Black Madonna. New York (Penguin Books).
Glasser, R. J. (1971): 365 Days. New York (George Braziller).
Gray, F. (1990): Soviet Women. Walking the Tightrope. New York (Anchor Books).
Griffin, S. (1978): Woman and Nature: The Roaring Inside Her. San Francisco (Harper Colophon).
Hallock, D. (1998): Hell, Healing and Resistance: Veteran's Speak. Farmington, PA (Plough Publishing House of the Bruderhof Foundation).
Heyneman, M. (1985): A Fine Upstanding Man. Parabola 10 (3): 18-25.
Houston, J. (1982): The Possible Human. Los Angeles (Tarcher).
Juhan, D.(1987): The Body of Life. New York (Knopf).
Kolga, M. (Ed.) (2002): The Red Book of the Peoples of the Russian Empire. Tallin, Estonia (Eesti Keele Instuut).
Koromila, M. (Ed.) (1992): The Greeks in the Black Sea from the Bronze Age to the Early 20th Century. Athens, Greece (The Panoramic Cultural Society).
Kramer, H. and J. Sprenger (1971): The Malleus Maleficarum (M. Summers, Trans.) New York (Dover) (Original work published in 1486).
Krippner, S. and B. Colodzin (1989): Multi-cultural Methods of Treating
Vietnam Veterans with Post-traumatic Stress Disorder. International journal of Psychosomatics 36 (1-4); 79-85.
Lifton, R. J. (1973) Home From the War. New York (Simon &

Schuster).
Lifton, R. J. (1979). The Broken Connection. New York (Simon & Schuster).
Merchant, C. (1980): The Death of Nature. New York (Harper & Row).
O'Brien, T. (1990): The Things They Carried. New York (Penguin).
Ornstein, R. (1986): The Pyschology of Consciousness. New York (Penguin), 3rd ed.
Paiva, I. (1989): The Lilith Factor: We Are Not All Children of Eve. New York (Penguin).
Pirsig, R. (1983): "Zen and the Art of Motorcycle Maintenance" in: S. Van Matre a. B. Weiler (Eds.): The Earth Speaks. Warrenville, IL (Illinois Institute for Earth Education).
Plaskow, J. and C. Christ (Eds.) (1972): Weaving the Visions. New Patterns in Feminist Spirituality. San Francisco (Harper & Row).
Progoff, I. (1975): At a Journal Workshop. New York (Dialogue House).
Sams, J. and D. Carson (1988): Medicine Cards. The Discovery of Power Through the Ways of Animals. Santa Fe, NM (Bear).
Sanchez, D. (2001): Sophia's Smile: Movement and Creativity in Healing and Transformation. (Ph. D. dissertation). Berkeley, CA (The Western Institute for Social Research).
Schacter, D. L. (1982): Stranger Behind the Engram. Theories of Memory and Psychology and Science. Hillsdale, N] (Lawrence Erlbaum).
Schwartz, H. (1988): Lilith's Cave: Jewish Tales of the Supernatural. San Francisco (Harper & Row).
Scott, M. H. (1991): The Passion of Being Woman. Aspen, CO (MacMurray & Beck Communications).
Severin, T (1986): The Jason Voyage. The Quest for The Golden Fleece. Ulverscroft, UK (Large Print Books).
Talbott, S. (1992): A Miracle Wrapped in Danger. TIME Magazine (December): 34-35.
Tamarov, V (1992): Afghanistan: Soviet Vietnam. San Francisco, CA (Mercury).
Thompson, W I. (1971): At the Edge of History. New York (Harper & Row).
Thompson, W I. (1978): Darkness and Scattered Light. New York (Anchor).
Thompson, W. I. (1981): The Time Falling Bodies Take to Light. New York (St. Martin's).

Thompson, W I. and D. Spangler (1991): Re-imagination of the World.
A Critique of the New Age, Science and Popular Culture. Santa Fe, NM (Bear).
Trevor-Roper, H. R. (1969): The European Witch Craze of the Sixteenth and Seventeenth Centuries and Other Essays. New York (Harper Torchbooks).
Webb, I. (1978): Fields of Fire. New York (Bantam).

Made in the USA
Middletown, DE
17 December 2019